The Man Who Was Shakespeare

For Vera . . . for the best of reasons

The Man Who Was Shakespeare

A SUMMARY OF
THE CASE UNFOLDED IN

*THE
MYSTERIOUS
WILLIAM SHAKESPEARE:
The Myth and the Reality*

Charlton Ogburn

EPM Publications, Inc.
McLean, Virginia

Library of Congress Cataloging-in-Publication Data

Ogburn, Charlton, 1911-
    The man who was Shakespeare : a summary of the case unfolded in
The mysterious William Shakespeare, the myth and the reality /
Charlton Ogburn.
        p.   cm.
    ISBN 0-939009-90-0
        1. Shakespeare, William, 1564-1616—Authorship—Oxford theory.
    2. Oxford, Edward De Vere, Earl of, 1550-1604—Authorship.
    3. Dramatists, English—Early modern, 1500-1700—Biography.
    4. Nobility—Great Britain—Biography.   I. Ogburn, Charlton, 1911-
    The mysterious William Shakespeare.   II. Title.
    PR2947. 090514   1995
    822.3'3—dc20
                                                    95-21081
                                                    CIP

EPM Publications, Inc., 1003 Turkey Run Road
    McLean, VA 22101
Printed in the United States of America

Cover and book design by Tom Huestis

To the Reader

This is a summary review of the investigation into the identity of our greatest writer pursued in *The Mysterious William Shakespeare: The Myth and the Reality.* (892 pp., 33 illus., 1984), Dodd, Mead, New York, N.Y.; second edition, amplified and enhanced, 1992, EPM Publications, McLean, Virginia.) The following pages set forth the most telling circumstances bearing upon the question of the authorship of Shakespeare's works as far as I have been able to incorporate them within the limited compass of this survey; and I hope that readers seeking further light on any particulars will consult the original work, in which will be found an extensive bibliography in addition to a detailed index and chronological tables of the period covered.

This exposition, compressed as it is, may be found rather demanding reading. However, the story of which it presents the highlights will, I believe, be found the greatest in the history of literature, and one of the most compelling ever, a life story on a par with the immortal Shakespearean dramas themselves—-which indeed, it tellingly imbues. From any accounts written of him, the dramatist is probably less known to the generality of readers than any other great writer at the same time that he is the best known of all as he stands revealed in the poems and plays that have gripped our imaginations for four centuries.

C. O.

"The man of letters is, in truth, ever writing his own biography. . . . And if he can so write that the world at large shall care to read what is written, no other memoir will perhaps be necessary."

ANTHONY TROLLOPE

AN AGE-OLD PUZZLE

Not long after William Shakspere of Stratford-on-Avon (Shakspere being the name under which he was baptized and buried) came to be celebrated as the immortal poet-dramatist, beginning in the 1740s, skepticism as to his credentials as such began to be voiced in print. In 1769, the very year in which the great actor David Garrick was staging a ground-breaking jubilee in Stratford, a physician friend of Garrick's brought out a book in which "Shakespeare" came by his gifts through robbing some travelers of their magic possessions. In 1786 appeared an historical allegory by "An Officer of the Royal Navy," which explained that "Shakespeare" had been one of a number of reincarnations of "Learned Pig." The name suggests Bacon, and Francis Bacon was for many years the preferred candidate of those seeking a more plausible Shakespeare than Will Shakspere of Stratford.

Bacon was, indeed, the explicit choice of the Reverend Dr. James Wilmot, a friend of Samuel Johnson's, who became rector in a village near Stratford-on-Avon in about 1781 and set about to learn all he could of the town's illustrious son. What he met with was a dearth of any reminders of the poet-dramatist. Though he combed the countryside for fifty miles around, he found not a single book that had belonged to such a one. While his findings were not to be published until 1932, he had decided that Sir Francis Bacon possessed the knowledge that Shakespeare commanded and that the Stratfordian could not have been "the real author." A decade earlier, another clergyman, Dr. Richard Graves, in a book about his rambles, recalled how in Warwickshire "All the idea which the country people have of that great genius [William Shakespeare] is that he excelled in smart repartee and in the selling of bargains, as they call it."

7

Because his testimony is likely to be found as of historic importance, we may go back over a hundred years to still another clergyman, Dr. John Ward, who became a vicar in Stratford-on-Avon in 1662. Recording in his notebook some details about "Shakespeare's" heirs, he wrote that "I have heard that Mr. Shakespeare was a natural wit without any art at all"—a statement doubtless as true of the Stratfordian as it was monstrously untrue of the greatest of all artists in words. Dr. Ward also wrote that "he supplied the stage with two plays every year, and for that had an allowance so large that he spent at the rate of £1000 a year, as I have heard." This is wildly out of line with any emoluments the Stratfordian could have received, let alone as an allowance, but it could be highly significant if found to be true of a more likely Shakespeare than the reputed "Bard." Although resolving to "be versed in" Shakespeare's plays and having Shakspere's granddaughter to sound out, Dr. Ward had not another word to say of Shakespeare in his additional sixteen notebooks, covering his nineteen years in Stratford.

The first overt rejection in print of the Shakespeare we are taught to believe in came in 1837 when, in a novel by Benjamin Disraeli, Lord Cadurcis, said to have been modeled on Lord Byron, expresses doubt that Shakespeare "ever wrote a single whole play." Thereafter, two outstanding heads of state familiar with the centers of power of which Shakespeare wrote so often, Lord Palmerston and Count Otto von Bismarck, spoke out in disbelief in the capacity of the Stratfordian to have done so, the former exulting—somewhat prematurely—in "the explosion of the Shakespearean illusion." John Bright, British statesman and Lord Rector of the University of Glasgow, avowed that "Any man who believes that William Shakespeare of Stratford wrote *Hamlet* or *Lear* is a fool."

To these disbelievers may be added distinguished men of law, specially trained in the evaluation of evidence, men like Lord Penzance and Sir George Greenwood, Member of Parliament and Queen's Counsel, in Britain; and, over here, Richard C. Bentley, former president of the Chicago Bar Association and editor of the *American Bar Association Journal;* W. Barton Leach, Story Professor of Law and David Cavers, Fessenden Professor of Law, both of Harvard; and three Justices of the U.S. Supreme Court, of whom Harry A. Blackmun and Lewis F. Powell, Jr., flatly rejected the Stratfordian and John Paul Stevens contrasted the credentials of the Stratfordian with those of the leading alternative candidate today to the clear disadvantage of the former (this in a lecture reprinted in the

University of Pennsylvania Law Review).

Among the iconoclasts have been outstanding writers deeply acquainted with the sources of literary creation. As for who "wrote the wonderful plays," John Greenleaf Whittier was "quite sure the man Shaksper neither did nor could." Walt Whitman was "firm against Shaksper—I mean the Avon man." Mark Twain confessed himself "the Brontosaurian" who "doesn't really know" who wrote the plays "but is quite composedly and contentedly sure that Shakespeare [that is, "the Avon man"] *didn't*." Henry James was "'sort of' haunted by the conviction that the divine William is the biggest and most successful fraud ever practiced on a patient world." Other novelists who have seen the Stratfordian as a fraud include John Galsworthy, Daphne duMaurier and Vladimir Nabokov. Charles Dickens wrote that "The life of Shakespeare is a fine mystery, and I tremble every day lest something should turn up." Ralph Waldo Emerson considered the identity of Shakespeare "the first of all literary problems." Prominent actors who have rejected the "Bard of Avon" are Sir Charles Chaplin, Leslie Howard, Sir Cedric Hardwicke, Orson Welles and Sir John Gielgud. The list includes also the veteran book-reviewer for *The New Yorker*, Clifton Fadiman. And in a class by himself, Sigmund Freud, whose candidate, like Fadiman's was the one to be forward in this paper. In the 1940s a professor at Northwestern University, Joseph S. Galland, compiled a bibliography of dissent from the conventional attribution of Shakespeare's works that came to six volumes in typescript and included over 4,500 items. By today the total has doubtless doubled or tripled.

Such impressive repudiation of the conventional attribution of the greatest literary works of our civilization—conventional in being backed by the vehement assurances of the academic scholars and their literary followers—is without parallel in the history of the arts. How is it to be accounted for?

There are two explanations, each sweeping.

In the first place, the Warwickshire Shakspere—and the family name clearly was not Shakespeare, with a long "a"—was in his background, character, education, or lack of it, opportunities and reputation while alive very nearly the antithesis of the kind of man we judge Shakespeare to have been on the testimony of his works. The world in which Shakespeare moved by consistent choice with naturalness and confidence was one to which the glover's son of Stratford would have had scant access; and that he brought this world convincingly to life is evident in the delight that three successive monarchs at its center took in his plays. The most determined, painstaking and sustained search has never turned up anything in Will Shakspere's writing but six crude signatures, all executed in the last four years of his life, and none but those on his will in Stratford, although the signatures of those with whom he did business in the town are by no means lacking. His parents, siblings, wife and daughters were illiterate except that one daughter could, like her father, sign her name. (Can we imagine the creator of Rosaline, Beatrice and Portia not teaching his daughters to write— or even to read his own peerless works?) The house in Stratford he owned during the last 19 years of his life remained in the possession of a daughter, later a granddaughter during the time three monumental editions of Shakespeare's plays were published, prefaced by 80 lines of poetical eulogy, the highest praise ever given a writer. Had Shakspere been Shakespeare, circumstances would have been especially propitious for the preservation of his literary effects, published and unpublished manuscripts and notes, letters he would have written his family. Yet nothing of the sort has ever come to light. W.W. Gregg was able to reproduce the holographs of 35 dramatists and 42 poets of Shakespeare's century but found none from the pen of the greatest of all. If Shakspere ever owned a single work of Shakespeare's there is no indication if it.

At the height of Shakspere's alleged fame, the London tax-collectors could not discover where he lived. He never, so far as is known, claimed to have written any of the works later ascribed to him or anything else. While ready enough to have an unfortunate surety jailed to avenge himself on a defaulting debtor and to hoard grain in time of famine, there is no record of his ever having made or sought to make a farthing from the immortal works now said to have been his or having taken a hand in their publication or having uttered a word of protest when they were pirated. Dying when 20 of the incomparable plays remained unprinted, he made no mention of them in his will and showed no interest in their survival. While Prospero in *The Tempest*, in whom, surely, we see the dramatist in a last appearance, avowed that "I loved my books" and could speak of "volumes that I prize above my dukedom," Shakspere's detailed will mentions not a book, and Professor T.W. Baldwin in his two-volume encomium to the Stratfordian's education (certainly one of the greatest feats of imagination ever offered as fact) ruefully concludes that "we have no absolutely conclusive external proof, so far as I know [read "no evidence at all"], that he ever owned a book of any kind." This, the man who invested money enough in three real-estate deals that we know of to have bought hundreds of books. Had Shakspere been the author, he would have been the most retarded poet of any stature known to history, having written no publishable verse before his late 20s. During his lifetime, no one we know of ever suggested that he was the dramatist William Shakespeare or a writer of any kind.

Ah, but, we are told, his career as an actor and theatrical manager stands warrant, along with his name, for his having been the dramatist. It may be conceded that he held theatrical properties. If so—and, curiously, there is no mention of his valuable shares in the Globe and Blackfriars in his will—a good guess is that he received them as part of the arrangement whereby he served as a stand-in for the dramatist while keeping out of sight of knowing Londoners. At the same time, there is nothing about Shakspere to suggest an actor; he was a mercenary, grasping, provincial business-man of whom nothing favorable was every said that we know of ex-cept that he had a wit. He was never while alive listed in the cast of any play yet discovered and there is no record of a part ever as-signed to him. The records of 70 municipalities in which players performed yield no mention of his or any similar name. Neither do the illuminating records kept by those two leading theatrical fig-ures, Philip Henslowe (who produced plays of Shakespeare's) and his son-in-law Edward Alleyn. Nor do any records of the reign of Elizabeth except one of a payment to "Will Kempe, Will Shake-speare & Richard Burbage servants to the Lord Chamberlain" for comedies performed before the Queen in December 1594. The entry is suspect on two counts, however. On one of the dates men-tioned, another company played before the Queen. And the pay-ment was reported long after the event by the harassed widow of the Treasurer of the Chamber whose late husband's books were three years in arrears and who, under Elizabeth's harsh imperative, had a sizable shortage in his accounts to make up for. But how did she happen to think of the name "Will Shakespeare"? The drama-tist, it would seem, found the stage so irresistible that he sneaked into plays and lost caste by doing so, even though he did so under his pseudonym—or so we may judge from a few lines of verse of 1610 by John Davies of Hereford. Addressed to "Our English Ter-rence, Mr. Wil. Shake-speare" (and note the hyphen) it tells us that had he "not played some kingly parts in sport," he had "been a companion for a king." That, by the way, is absolutely all we know about the kind of actor Shakespeare was; and of course any notion that the busy professional actor from Stratford of legend would have played his parts in sport, and would have lowered himself by playing kingly parts or would in any circumstances have been a companion for a king is of course ludicrous. When we speak of Shakespeare we are speaking of a man of whom those things were clearly true. And it was his shadowy figure as an actor, we may believe, that in part was responsible for William Shakespeare's being listed twice on the accession of King James among the Lord Chamberlain's players, thenceforth to be known as the King's Men.

In the near-total absence of material for a life of Shakspere as Shakespeare, his partisans have come to take two related testaments as the cornerstone of their biographies. One is *Groats-worth of Wyt*, published in 1592 as the work of the dying Robert Greene, who is represented as warning his fellow playwrights of an unnamed actor. The other is an expression of regret by Henry Chettle for printing *Groatsworth* inasmuch as one of the playwrights, who had taken offense at it, had turned out to be a polished and respected writer. The academicians insist that both the slandered actor and the offended playwright were the Stratfordian "Shakespeare," but no one we know of thought so for two centuries and, as we shall see when we come to these proceedings later, there is no reason whatever for believing so now.

We may let Robert Bearman sum up for us. As he wrote in *Shakespeare in the Stratford Records* (1994), published by the Shakespeare Birthplace Trust:

> Certainly there is little, if anything, to remind us that we are studying the life of one who in his writings emerges as perhaps the most gifted of all time in describing the human condition. Here in Stratford he seems merely to have been a man of the world, buying up property, laying in ample stocks of barley and malt, when others were starving, selling off his surpluses and pursuing debtors in court, and conniving, as it seems, in the Welcombe enclosures. . . .

perhaps the most gifted of all time in describing the human condition.

Mr. Bearman may serve also to introduce us to the other grounds for dismissing the claims made for the Stratfordian .

The Pre-Eminence of Shakespeare—the Elusive

"Look you," the German poet Heinrich Heine declared, "the good God himself naturally has a right to the first place, but the second certainly belongs to Shakespeare." Few persons, I suspect, would dispute Heine's judgment that Shakespeare's was the greatest creative mind, certainly in the written word, of all mortals. His fellow playwright, John Dryden, writing in 1668, called William Shakespeare "the man who of all modern, and perhaps ancient, poets, had the largest and most comprehensive soul" and hailed him as "divine." His was "the greatest of intellects" to Thomas Carlyle, who declared that "there is actually a kind of sacredness in the fact of such a man being sent to this earth." Algernon Charles Swinburne could exclaim, "There is one book in the world of which it might be affirmed . . . that it would be better for the world to lose all others and keep this one than to lose this and keep all other treasures bequeathed by human genius to all that we can conceive of eternity." And he added, "The word Shakespeare connotes more than any other man's name that ever was written or spoken upon earth."

Probably there is never a day on which a score of Shakespeare's plays are not somewhere being staged. They have been translated into every language capable of serving as a vehicle for them. Without them, our society would be a different and much impoverished one. Shakespeare's phrases come continually to our minds, even to the speech of those who have never read him, to express our meaning better and more trenchantly than we can on our own. *Bartlett's Familiar Quotations* (1980) contains nine times more pages of Shakespeare than of the runner-up—John Milton—and almost twice as many as of the Bible, the work of a congeries of writers. His characters, their names familiar on our lips as household words (slightly to paraphrase the master)—Hamlet, Polonius and Gertrude, Portia and Shylock, Macbeth and Lady Macbeth, Henry the Fifth and Falstaff, Romeo and Juliet—are among the immortals who accompany us through life, as intimately realized as if we had known them.

It can hardly be doubted that Shakespeare's contemporaries were as responsive to his poems and plays, as aware of his genius, as their descendants were to be; the Elizabethans were a cultivated, sophisticated lot, England's first great literary generation. The first two publications adorned with the name "William

Shakespare," *Venus and Adonis* and *The Rape of Lucrece*, were so popular that the former was to go through ten printings by 1602, the latter four (probably larger) by 1607. Previously, writing of a play unmistakably *Henry the Sixth, Part 1*, Thomas Nashe said that it had "moved to tears . . . ten thousand spectators at least (at several times)." The first known mention of Shakespeare as a playwright, in 1598, called him the best of the English for both comedy and tragedy. (Mysteriously, though at least 14 of his plays had been performed and/or printed, their author had remained unnamed.) The eulogist went on to declare that "The Muses would speak with Shakespeare's fine-filed phrase if they would speak English." In 1623 he was paid the unheard-of tribute of having his collected plays published, in the famous First Folio. In an introductory poem to the volume, the leading literary figure of the time, Ben Jonson, proclaimed him the "Soul of the Age,/ The applause! delight! the wonder of our stage," Britain's triumph who "was not of an age but for all time" and who "so did take Eliza and our James"— the latter having had seven of his plays produced in the aftermath of his coronation in 1604. (When Jonson had had his own collected plays published in 1616 he was ridiculed for his pretension.)

Surely other writers, actors, university men, courtiers would have sought the acquaintance of such a man as Shakespeare was. Yet no one we know of reported in the years when he was alive ever to have met, seen or had any communication with a poet or dramatist named William Shakespeare, and only three did so even years after his death. The actors Heminge and Condell were represented as calling him "so worthy a friend and fellow" without attributing a single personal characteristic to him and Ben Jonson could find none other than that he was "honest, and of an open and free nature"—the only picture he left us of the immortal Shakespeare he "loved on this side idolatry." Can we doubt that the poet-dramatist was known, where known, in a different identity and that "William Shakespeare" was a mask for a man of high station who would have been a companion for a king had he not played kingly parts in sport? Can it be otherwise than that by hyphenating the name "Shake-speare" as often as not, his contemporaries were indicating that they recognized it as a made-up one, like Shakespeare's own Master Shoe-tie and Master Starve-lackey. And why would the dramatist have chosen the *non de plume* he did? Perhaps for one reason because *Hasti-vibrfans*, the Spear-shaker, was the sobriquet of Pallas Athena, who was said to have sprung from the brow of Zeus fully armed and brandishing a spear; and

Pallas Athena was the patron goddess of Athens, home of the theatre.

Stratfordians may argue that in fact Shakespeare did not receive the plaudits to have been expected from his fellows had they perceived him as we do. If so, there is plainly a reason having nothing to do with recognition of his genius. Addressing "Mr. William Shake-speare," an epigrammist of 1640 wrote:

> Shake-speare, we must be silent in thy praise,
> 'Cause our encomiums will but blast thy bays;
> Which envy could not, that thou didst so well;
> Let thine own histories prove thy chronicle.

We can only guess why encomiums should deprive Shake-speare of the laurel wreath traditionally crowning poets, but it is clear that his contemporaries were inhibited from openly praising him. The last line of the verse should guide us in our quest: Let Shake-speare's plays tell us his story. The principle is one that has been repeatedly enunciated. As Jean de la Fontaine observed, "By the work one knows the workman." Anatole France spoke to similar effect in declaring that "The artist either communicates his own life to his creations or else merely whittles out puppets and dresses up dolls." So did Samuel Butler, who wrote that "Every man's work whether it be literature or music or pictures or architecture or anything else is always a portrait of himself." A man's "work is autobiographical in spite of every subterfuge," said the poet Wallace Stevens.

What, then, does Shakespeare tell us of himself in his works?

"Most Like A Noble Lord"

It cannot escape notice that of the 37 plays of the Shakespeare canon, 36 are laid in royal courts and the world of the nobility or otherwise in the highest realm of society. (The word "noble" appears some 650 times in the plays.) The one variant, *The Merry Wives of Windsor,* is surely of them all the most forced and unsatisfactory. The principal characters are for the rest almost all aristocratic, even the young man who wins the beautiful Anne Page in *The Merry Wives.* Shylock is an exception, but that galvanic figure stands altogether outside the social order. Falstaff would seem to be another, but he is a familiar of the peerage and a close companion of a prince; yet even he at the end is spurned by the prince, now a king, and humiliated. No other dramatist before or since has drawn his casts so predominately from the nobility or been such a literary habitué of successive English courts.

From all we can tell, moreover, Shakespeare fully shared the lordly outlook of his principal character. "An aristocrat born," Frank Harris recognized in him, one who "felt in himself a kinship for the courtesies, chivalries, and generousness of aristocratic life." Such is surely the author called up in our minds by his works "Conceived out of the fullest heat and pulse of European feudalism," as Walt Whitman put it, speaking specifically of the historical plays, "only one of the wolfish earls so plenteous in the plays themselves, or some born descendant and knower, might seem to have been the author of those amazing works—works in some respects greater than anything else in recorded history."

"The heavens themselves, the planets, and this centre," Ulysses declares in *Troilus and Cressida*, "Observe degree, priority, and place, . . ." with the sun ruling as king: "And therefore is the glorious planet Sol,/ In noble eminence enthroned and sphered amongst the others." And he goes on to describe the horrors that must follow "when degree is slaked." Bertram in *Cymbeline* leaves no doubt of Shakespeare's belief in social distinctions:

> Though mean and mighty rotting
> Together, leaving but one dust, yet reverence—
> That angel of the world—doth make distinction
> Of place, 'tween high and low.

The distinction is not to be blurred: Isabella in *Measure for Measure* explains that "Great men may jest with saints; 'tis wit in them,/ But, in the less, foul profanation." The fastidious patrician in Shakespeare speaks as the Duke in the same play: "I love the people,/ But do not like to stage me to their eyes." Coriolanus is a nobleman too proud even for Shakespeare. "When he walks, he moves like an engine, and the ground shrinks before his treading," we are told. "He wants nothing of a god but eternity." The play is pointedly revealing of the dramatist. "Sir, it is no little thing to make/ Mine eyes sweat with compassion," he has his protagonist confess to his foil Aufidius. And it is compassion, not pride, that brings Coriolanus down. Yet he is given the last word, as voiced by Aufidius, who on his death proclaims, "Let him be regarded/ As the most noble corse that ever herald/ Did follow to his urn."

It is especially telling that when Coriolanus is banished for his contemptuous arrogance by the populace ("You common cry of curs, whose breath I hate," he avows) the populace is shown to have erred by upsetting the divine order and must pay for it: they respected not the gods, they are told, "and he, returning to break our necks, they respect not us." "Giddy and unsure" is the popular will in Shakespeare. As Octavius Caesar expresses it:

> The common body
> Like to vagabond flag [iris] upon the stream,
> Goes back and forth, lackeying the varying tide,
> To rot itself with motion.

The rabble-rousing, popular rebel-leader, Jack Cade, himself voices a similar complaint of his following: "Was ever feather blown so lightly to and fro as this multitude?"

Lower-class characters in Shakespeare are almost all introduced for comic effect and given scant development in their own right; as Walt Whitman observes, they "serve as capital foils to the aristocracy." Their names bespeak their inferior worth: Snug, Bottom, Stout, Starveling, Dogberry, Simple, Mouldy, Wart, Feeble, Bullcalf, Mistress Quickly and Doll Tearsheet. "The comedies (exquisite as they certainly are)," Whitman resumes, "are altogether unacceptable to America and Democracy"; but Shakespeare could not withhold his genius even from "these admirably portrayed common characters," and he gives to Feeble, for example, some lines I could least part with (lines I shall come to). As for that essential medium of popular rule, the politician, Shakespeare did not conceal his scorn. Lear says:

> Get thee glass eyes;
> And like a scurvy politician seem
> To see things thou dost not.

"What infinite heart's ease," Henry V exclaims, "/Must kings neglect that private men enjoy!" Not all the pomp and ceremony "laid in bed majestical,/ Can sleep so soundly as the wretched slave." What can scarcely be overlooked in Shakespeare is a compassionate understanding of the burdens of kingship combined with envy of the supposedly carefree lot of the peasant, who free of the "peril" of the "envious court," "sweetly . . . enjoys his thin cold drink" and his "sleep under a fresh tree's shade" with

17

"no enemy but winter and rough weather." This would come naturally to a privileged nobleman familiar at first hand with the anguish the crown can bring but remote from the realities of the ploughman's life of toil and want.

"Knowledge the Wing Wherewith We Fly"

"Good sportsmen, like good men, are rarer than bad, . . . and among the best of the 16th century we must certainly rank William Shakespeare." The quotation is from a remarkable, two-volume work, *Shakespeare's England*, to which an array of specialists contribute to 30 chapters on the "Life and Manners" of the Elizabethan age. There are nearly 100 pages on sports, chiefly those that only the nobility had the means of practicing, the whole chapter liberally illustrated with quotations from Shakespeare. One would judge the dramatist to have been a master horseman, while falconry repeatedly supplied him with images. Familiar with hunting to hounds, he must have been a rarity in his times in the sympathy he expresses for the wounded quarry.

The 1,100 pages of *Shakespeare's England* bring out the awesome extent of the dramatist's grasp and evocation of the world around him, as illustrated by the more than 2,300 quotations from his works (according to a special index). No other writer of the time, we may be sure, had such a range. He can only have been one of the best educated men of his generation. In language skills he stands alone. Where the average well-educated person today is said by the philologist Max Müller to use about 4,000 words, Shakespeare is credited by Alfred Hart of the University of Melbourne with a vocabulary of 17,677 twice the size of Milton's. Professor Hart observes that "a writer who has 12,000 words at his command each of which he uses in no more than four plays and is credited by the compilers of the *Oxford English Dictionary* with being the first user of about 3,200 words . . . has verbal riches compelling the employment of superlatives in describing them." In a 400-page study Sister Miriam Joseph, C.S.S., shows "how Shakespeare used the whole body of logical-rhetorical knowledge of his time. The Elizabethan mystery-man was not only a master of the language but a peerless enhancer of it, one whose contribution to our phraseology, according to another noted philologist, Ernest

Weekly, "is ten times greater than that of any other writer to any language."

Scholars like William Allen Neilson and Ashley Horace Thorndike have listed background works in English Shakespeare must have been acquainted with, and an impressive assortment it is. They testify, too, to his familiarity with both the Genevan and Great Bibles while Charles Wadsworth, Bishop of St. Andrews, writes: "Put together our best authors, who have written on subjects not professedly religious or theological, and we shall not find, I believe, in them *all united*, so much evidence of the Bible having been read and used, as we have found in Shakespeare alone."

Qualified scholars tell us that Shakespeare could and did read Greek and Latin classics in the original. (Professor Churtin Collins is—reluctantly—confident that Shakespeare had read the *Ajax* of Sophocles: "Reminiscences of it seem to haunt his dramas.") Transferring Shakespeare's acquaintance with classical literature to the Stratfordian, Professor T.W. Baldwin requires two volumes to account for the schooling needed to have produced it. Professor Charles Tyler Prouty in a publication by the Yale University Press assures us that Shakespeare "read both Italian and French"; his plays show a familiarity with outstanding writers in both languages.

Two centuries ago the Shakespearean scholar, and lawyer, Edmund Malone, wrote of his subject that "His knowledge of legal terms is not merely such as might be acquired by the casual observation of even his all-comprehending mind; it has the appearance of technical skill." Ever since then lawyers have been exclaiming over Shakespeare's professional knowledge of their field. In the mid-19th Century, Lord Chief Justice John Campbell wrote that the dramatist had a "deep technical knowledge of the law" and an easy familiarity "with some of the most abstruse proceedings in English jurisprudence." His contemporary, Sir John Plaisted Wilde, Lord Penzance, holder of high judicial posts, declared in a eulogy of Shakespeare's legal accomplishments: "At every turn and point at which the author required a metaphor, simile or illustration, his mind ever turned first to the law."

At the same time, John Bucknill in a book entitled *The Medical Knowledge of Shakespeare* undertook to show that his subject's understanding of medicine was the most advanced of his, Bucknill's own, time and embraced the more intelligent treatments of the insane of that same time. It was the start of repeated testimonials to Shakespeare's knowledge of medicine. This, according to Dr. Samuel M. Dodek of the George Washington School of Medicine, qualified him "to hang out his shingle as an Elizabethan M.D." Dr. Frank N. Miller, Jr., of the same faculty, found "a dazzling array of over 1400 medical references in Shakespeare's dramas and poems," of which the Australian physician Dr. Aubrey C. Kail, in a book devoted to *The Medical Knowledge of Shakespeare*, observed that the plays "bear witness to a profound knowledge of contemporary physiology and psychology." "Shakespeare was the greatest analyst of all," Dr. Daniel E. Schneider declared, adding that "the so-called authentic Shakespeare could not possibly have written the plays. It seems to me that he was a front-man for somebody else."

The point should be made that Shakespeare does not display his familiarity with a subject merely when writing about that subject. He does not bone up on one to parade his knowledge of it, as Ben Jonson does. His learning comes out almost of itself. The law, as Edgar I. Fripp observes, is so much a part of him that it "slips from him unawares." Without his writing "about" medicine, "Medical images," as Dr. Dodek notes, "heighten the atmosphere of his plays, especially the tragedies," which "are suffused with pathology." Othello draws on falconry to make vivid his suspicion of Desdemona, Juliet her attachment to Romeo. To make poignant the king's insomnia, Shakespeare calls up "the wet sea-boy" falling asleep on the masthead. It is to characterize her fun-loving Antony that Cleopatra recalls the disporting dolphin.

Images of the sea, we may in turn recall, are recurrent in Shakespeare. Indeed, Lieutenant Commander A.F. Falconer of the Royal Navy concludes that "knowledge of the sea and the Navy can be seen from his earliest plays." He is particularly aware of "the fatal bowels of the deep," as Richard III speaks of them. To be insatiable was to Shakespeare to be "as hungry as the sea" the "never-surfeited sea." Joseph Conrad felt that the ultimate characterization of the element with which he had contested in his years as a mariner was in the phrase with which Iago is cursed upon Othello's death, "more fell than anguish, hunger or the sea." At the same time the martial element is so pronounced in the plays as to suggest a special pre-occupation with military affairs on the dramatist's part, and the suspicion is reinforced by his characters' convincing evocation of the deadly but heady drama of the field; think of Hotspur's wrathful disgust in *Henry the Fourth, Part 1,* at the mincing lord who came to demand his prisoners of him (it was a favorite passage of General Joseph W. Stilwell's); of Othello's glorification of the combat he was forsaking, beginning "Farewell the plumèd troop and the big wars that/ Make ambition virtue"; of Henry V exhorting his troops to a supreme endeavor in the teeth of the enemy.

If in such vignettes the dramatist was romanticizing a past, it was otherwise in lines he gave the raw recruit, Feeble, in *Henry the Fourth, Part 2.* In his anthology entitled *Men at War*, of 1942, Ernest Hemingway recalls them as affording "a permanent protecting talisman" when, at 19, a young British officer in the hospital wrote them out for him:

"By my troth, I care not; a man can die but once; we owe God a death . . . and let it go which way it will, he that dies this year is quit for the next." To Hemingway, "That is probably the best thing that is written in this book, and, with nothing else a man can get along all right on that."

No one long given to the observation of nature can fail to be struck by Shakespeare's astuteness in it. We find him noticing that the lapwing runs in a crouch and that the cuckoo's favorite victim is the hedge-sparrow, and we see with his eyes the choughs "Rising and cawing at the gun's report" to "sever themselves and madly sweep the skies" and how the sun "fires the proud tops of the eastern pines." His love of and knowledge of flowers wild and domestic cannot be overlooked; two beautifully illustrated books have been written on it and a garden in Central Park in Manhattan given over to flowers he mentions. He knew "the bank whereon the wild thyme blows,/ Where oxlips and the nodding violet grows./ Quite over-canopied with luscious woodbine,/ With sweet musk-roses, and with eglantine." He knew and touched with poetry the flowers of spring, "daffodils,/ That come before the swallow dares" and "violets dim,/ But sweeter than the lids of Juno's eyes; pale primroses. . . ." and the flowers of summer: "Hot lavender, mints, savory, marjoram;/ The marigold that goes to bed wi' the sun." *The Birds of Shakespeare* by James E. Harting, F.L.S., F.Z.S., examines and illustrates at book-length "The Ornithology of Shakespeare." Have we not in the poet-dramatist a privileged gentleman with a country seat? (In his elegantly illustrated *Shakespeare's Birds*, of 1983, Peter Goodfellow asserts that Shakespeare knew so much about falconry, using "naturally and accurately . . . so many technical terms that he must have been involved, perhaps on visits to one of his noble friends.")

Equally evident in Shakespeare is, surely, an addiction to and love of music. He warns us of the man that hath not music in his soul and invokes the magic of music 130 times in the plays; he uses a hundred musical terms. At the same time he has inspired more music by far than any other writer, Berlioz, Mendelssohn, Verdi, Tchaikovsky and Prokofiev having given major musical settings to his works (and not forgetting Cole Porter's obeisance to Shakespeare in *Kiss Me Kate*).

The hold the Continent had on Shakespeare stands out in his plays. Of all those taking place in his own times, only one, the ill-favored *Merry Wives of Windsor* again, is laid in England. All the others have Europe as their scene, Italy above all. "As soon as I reached the northern provinces of Italy, I was constantly being reminded of Shakespeare," Gilbert Highet, a man of unimpeachable orthodoxy, recalls. Dr. Ernesto Grillo in his *Shakespeare and Italy* says of *The Merchant of Venice* that "the topography is so precise and accurate that it must convince even the most superficial reader that the poet visited the country." To this, Pietro Rebora in his *L'Italia nella Drama Inglese* adds that Shakespeare "possessed a profound knowledge of Italian language and culture, of which he made an amazing use in the plays." There is no shortage of such testimony. Speaking of Shakespeare's "series of plays with Italian settings, which was something of a new departure in English drama," the dean of orthodox Shakespearean scholarship, Sir Edmund K. Chambers, himself concedes that his subject "even . . . shows familiarity with some minute points of local topography." Surely the trail we are following must lead to a dramatist with first-hand acquaintance with the towns of northern Italy that provide his scenes. Add to this Professor George Lyman Kittredge's judgment that "The influence of the Italian *commedia dell' arte* is visible throughout the play"—*Love's Labour's Lost*—and that "Several of the characters correspond to standard figures of the Italian convention," and we must find unaccountable that these works could be attributed by sane, respectable scholars to a raw recruit from a near bookless Warwickshire town.

What else? Shakespeare wrote of the circulation of the blood before Harvey announced its discovery. He located the drawing power of the earth at "its very center" a century before Newton had enunciated his principle of gravity (Shakespeare's use of the possessive pronoun "its," by the way, being the first known). He had mountains being leveled and the continent melting into the sea two centuries before James Hutton postulated that in the absence of countervailing forces, this is indeed how they would end. Three centuries before the term was invented, his Friar Laurence enunciated the basic principle of ecology in declaring in part, "For nothing so vile that on the earth doth live/ But to the earth some special good doth give." In a society that assumed that the natural world was designed as a supportive setting for man, Shakespeare could have been speaking, four centuries later, as a contemporary of our own in having Jaques repine

> that we
> Are mere usurpers, tyrants, and what's worse,
> To fright the animals and kill them up
> In their assigned and native dwelling place.

Here I may interrupt myself to note that Stratfordians make a crucial issue of the blunders they accuse Shakespeare of making, proving to their satisfaction that he could not have been a university man. Most of those on which they pounce are anachronisms. To these Shakespeare and his contemporaries were indifferent, much as if the past, insofar as it remained alive, were part of the present. No one was bothered that Rembrandt depicted Aristotle and Diana as burghers of Amsterdam, and certainly Shakespeare knew that Aristotle, whom he cites in *Troilus and Cressida*, came long after the siege of Troy. He might have observed, moreover, that if we were going to have the Romans guilty of the supreme anachronism of speaking English we might as well have them hear a clock striking. Two boners of which the academicians accuse Shakespeare with special zeal are in his making the painter Giulio Romano a sculptor and in endowing Bohemia with a seacoast. They have not troubled to learn that Romano, in his vanished epitaph, was proclaimed "corpora sculpta" (and how Shakespeare would have known that is enlightening in itself) and that in Shakespeare's time the Kingdom of Bohemia comprised the Archduchy of Austria, which bordered the Adriatic between the territories of the Venetian Republic. I do not mean to imply, however, that Shakespeare would have cared a fig whether Bohemia bordered the sea. "A foolish consistency," Emerson declared, "is the hobgoblin of little minds." And Shakespeare did not scruple to have a lion in the Forest of Arden when it suited his purpose. Stratfordians never call him to account for this, presumably because even a grammar-school drop-out, as was their Shakespeare, would have known that a lion in the forest of Arden, even if it was in France (i.e., the Ardennes) was not bloody likely.

"Having There My Verse, In Witness"

Up to now we have sought to derive a portrait of the author from his plays. In his sequence of 154 sonnets we have his direct, self-revelatory, albeit highly elliptical, testimony in the first person. What can we learn from them of his circumstances?

To begin with, the timing of the *Sonnets'* composition is important. The evidence is strong that it began with the publication of *Venus and Adonis* and *The Rape of Lucrece*, in 1593 and '94 respectively and continued until not long after 1603. In that year, in a sonnet clearly referring to events consequent upon the passing of Elizabeth, the poet recognized that "death to me subscribes." Most of the sequence clearly belongs to the earlier years. The majority are addressed to a young man of notable beauty and appeal. The two long narrative poems both bore a dedication to the Earl of Southampton, signed by William Shakespeare. These were the only times we know of when the author employed that name, and it did not appear on the title-pages. The dedications were couched in the courtly language of one gentleman addressing another, and the terms of remarkable devotion the young earl elicits in the dedication to *Lucrece* are nearly identical with those in which the young friend of the *Sonnets* is addressed. There can be but little doubt that the recipient of the poet's devotion in the two cases was the same—and all three of Southampton's biographers agree that this is so.

The *Sonnets* tell us that the poet:

—Was in his declining years when writing them. He was "Beated and chopped with tanned antiquity," "With Time's injurious hand crushed and o'er-worn," in the "twilight" of life. He is lamenting "all those friends" who have died, "my lovers gone." His is "That time of year/ When yellow leaves, or none, or few, do hang/ Upon those boughs that shake against the cold." One would think he cannot have been born much after 1550.

—Was of such position that he could address a young earl in terms of intimate endearment and longing. ("Dear my love"; "And thou hast all the all of me.")

—Could take a paternal attitude toward the young earl: as A.L. Rowse has observed, stood with relation to him in loco parentis. While confessing a self-abnegating devotion ("Lord of my love, to whom in vassalage/ Thy merit hath my duty strongly knit"), he chides him as a father might ("You to your beauteous blessings add a curse,/ Being fond on praise") and takes him scathingly to task ("O, what a mansion have those vices got,/ Which for their habitation chose out thee," and "Thy odour matcheth not thy show. . . . Thou dost common grow." It is very much the voice of a doting, exacting parent.

—Was a man who materially had lost, not gained, in life. He knew what it was to be "in disgrace with fortune and men's eyes." He was "made lame by fortune's dearest spite"; it is a recurrent theme.

—Lost caste by writing, presumably by writing for the public theatre. He exclaims:

Thence comes it that my name receives a brand,
And almost thence my nature is subdued
To what it works in, like the dyer's hand.

He says, "For I am shamed by that which I bring forth," and adds, "And so should you, to love things nothing worth." (Southampton was known to have felt the fascination of the theatre and was observed to neglect court-attendance because of it.)

—Had reason to believe that while his verse would be immortal, oblivion would be his own lot. He promises the young friend that:

When all the breathers of this world are dead:
You still shall live—such virtue hath my pen.
. . . Your praise shall still find room,
Even in the eyes of all posterity.

At the same time:

. . . I, once gone, to all the world must die;
The earth can yield me but a common grave.

The poet must certainly have expected that the *Sonnets* when printed would be dedicated to the object of his devotion just as the two narrative poems had been; otherwise it would have made no sense for him to exclaim, "Your name from hence immortal life shall have." Presumably he expected to sign the dedication, like its predecessors, with not his real name but doubtless, again, "William Shakespeare." Were the name to have been actually his own he could not have lamented that he "once gone, to all the world must die." Moreover, we read in another sonnet:

> That every word doth almost tell my name,
> Showing their birth and whence they did proceed.

If every word almost tells his name, it could only be that his name was not otherwise known—and we have the poet's own warrant for seeking his identity in his writings.

Finally, as we shall see presently, there is a particularly plain disclosure of the poet's noble rank in Sonnet 125.

Closing In On the Perpetrator

Let us now see if further inquiry into the evidence will lead us to a specific nobleman of whom those things we have inferred about Shakespeare will also be true, and uniquely so. We might think of ourselves as Elizabethan detectives seeking to identify the perpetrator of a crime of whom they know nothing except that he had adopted the pen-name William Shakespeare and had written the works that appeared under it. As such we should, of course, recognize that a nobleman writing for the public theatre would have been required by the *mores* of his class to conceal his authorship; even signing his published verse would be *infra dignitatis* for such a one. This was a nobleman, moreover, who did even worse than writing plays for the theatres then appearing in London. As we have seen, he was so addicted to the stage that he could not resist appearing on it surreptitiously under his pseudonym, at least in parts consonant with his station. How widely he was recognized, we do not know, but his actions would have been reported to the throne by the ubiquitous secret service, with consequences for his standing at Court.

Although *Venus and Adonis* was the first composition to which the name Shakespeare was appended, it had to have been preceded by less mature verse. So we should look for a nobleman who wrote youthful verse, and verse suggestive of Shakespeare's, we must hope under his own name. A man at home in the Court and a familiar figure there yet in his life apart an incomparable genius in literature would surely have been held a strange, unaccountable sort, temperamental, probably difficult, certainly controversial. His connection with the theatre must have been a close one, and he would necessarily have been drawn to other writers and playwrights, some of whom would presumably have known him for who he was; and having the greatest of their art in their midst, they could scarcely have failed to give some witness of it. We must look for a nobleman highly, if elliptically, praised by his fellow writers.

Then consider the historical plays, to which Walt Whitman paid such exalted tribute. Could this almost incredible treasure of drama have been composed with such passionate intensity and conviction, such sure instinct, such immense evocative power, unless the past it brought so vitally to life made somehow an irresistible claim upon the author?

We should look for self-portraits among Shakespeare's characters. If, as detectives, we are on to the ways of writers of imagined worlds, we may find the dramatist in youth on stage as Berowne in *Love's Labour's Lost*, Bertram in *All's Well that Ends Well* (with his faults faced up to), Benedick in *Much Ado About Nothing*, and Faulconbridge in *King John*—young gallants all drawn to military exploit. With added years and a more poetical nature laced with melancholy, he becomes Romeo (whose "mind misgives/ Some consequence yet hanging in the stars.") In him, we begin to recognize the guise in which every thoughtful reader must perceive the author most fully and intimately revealed, the Prince of Denmark, the most unforgettable character in literature. We should look among those close to the Queen for Hamlet.

Having deduced so much about the transgressor who had written Shakespeare's works, would our Elizabethan detectives be prepared to serve their warrant? Yes, undoubtedly. They would have descended without hesitation upon the poet pronounced "most excellent" of those of the Court by a critic in 1586; whom the playwright Anthony Munday, at one time his secretary, would someday warmly recall as a man of "matchless virtues," whom the poet George Chapman called "the most goodly fashioned man I ever saw, . . . of spirit passing great"; of whom, at 28, the noted university figure Gabriel Harvey proclaimed that "Phoebus Apollo has cultivated thy mind in the arts"; of whom Robert Greene had written that he stood in respect of other writers as Atalanta to hunters, Sappho to poets—in other words, the best of them all. And the reasoning we have had the detectives follow, it should be said, is similar to that which in 1920 led an English schoolmaster, J. Thomas Looney (who impatiently refused to change his name at the behest of a publisher), to set forth in his enthralling book, *"Shakespeare" Identified in Edward de Vere, Seventeenth Earl of Oxford.*

27

John Galsworthy called it "the best detective story I have ever read," and Sigmund Freud wrote the author, "The man of Stratford . . . seems to have nothing at all to justify his claim, whereas Oxford has almost everything."

Filling Out of the Picture

What put Looney on to the object of his quest to begin with was a search through an anthology of 16th century English poetry for a poem in the verse-form of *Venus and Adonis*, which he felt the poet had probably used in earlier, shorter lyrics. (The verse-form is also that of the last six lines—the sestet—of the Shakespearean sonnet.) The historic moment arrived with his coming upon a poem of three stanzas entitled "Women" by Edward de Vere, Earl of Oxford. Of this, the middle stanza reads:

> To mark the choice they make and how they change,
> How oft from Phoebus do they fly to Pan,
> Unsettled still like haggards wild they range,
> These gentle birds that fly from man to man,
> Who would not scorn and shake them from the fist
> And let them fly, fair fools, which way they list.

(Haggards are falcons captured as adults as distinguished from eyases, which are taken from the nest. "Fool" was used by Shakespeare as a term of endearment and pity.) "From Phoebus . . . to Pan" takes us, of course, to Hamlet's "from Hyperion to a satyr"; and, indeed, the poem is expressive of Hamlet's misgiving about women. The stanza is, too, clearly a precursor of Othello's lines:

> If I do prove her haggard,
> Though her jesses were my dear heart-strings,
> I'd whistle her and let her down the wind,
> To prey at fortune.

{Jesses are thongs attached to a falcon's legs by the trainer.)

From the poem "Women," Looney turned soon to the *Dictionary of National Biography* and to the De Veres, among whom he quickly found Edward, the 17th Earl of Oxford. Ironically, it was Sir Sydney Lee, outstanding orthodox Shakespearean scholar, who in his article in the *Dictionary*, of which he was editor, and in his *A Life of William Shakespeare*, supplied Looney with the initial information that showed Edward de Vere as meeting convincingly the criteria Looney had set up to satisfy him that he had the man who was Shakespeare.

Who was this man to whom the trail has led?

Edward de Vere: His Background and Youth

The de Veres came in with William the Conqueror. Soon Earls of Oxford, they were involved with all the monarchs who tread the boards in Shakespeare's historical plays. The 2nd Earl stood by King John, the 3rd was among the barons who curbed his powers. The 6th fought under the three successive Edwards,*. the 7th beside "that black name, Edward, Black Prince of Wales"—as the French king calls him in *Henry the Fifth*—at Crécy. The 9th was an intimate of Richard II's with—thanks to shared faults of character—-consequences fatal to both. The 11th Earl held an important command at Agincourt. The 13th—"brave Oxford, wondrous well-belov'd," as he is in Shakespeare—was a mainstay of the Lancastrian side so clearly favored by the dramatist, in the Wars of the Roses; on the battlefield of Bosworth ("See, where Oxford comes!") he helped bring down the super-villain (as Shakespeare portrays him), Richard III.

Edward de Vere was born on April 22 (new style), 1550 at Castle Hedingham in Essex. This had been the family seat since it had been built in 1140, and the 80-foot-high keep still stands today atop a hill above the picturesque village bearing the castle's name. At nine years old, so precocious was he, Edward matriculated at Queens' College, Cambridge.

In 1561, in her third year on the throne, Elizabeth had come to visit the 16th Earl at Castle Hedingham. Then nearing her 28th birthday, she was a handsome, vivacious young woman of outstanding intellect, proficient in Latin and Greek and in French, Italian and Spanish, and I like to believe that something like an electric current was set up between her and Edward. The eleven-year-old, we may observe, was already Viscount Bulbeck bearing as his crest a lion brandishing a broken spear. Her visit lasted from

---

* The play *Edward the Second* was, it seems clear, derived from a draft by Edward de Vere turned over to be completed by Christopher Marlowe, who would seem to have been a protégé of his and to whom the play is generally attributed, though it is quite out of line with his other works. Stratfordians have it that the play's similarity to Shakespeare's early historical dramas shows how the greater writer was indebted to the lesser.

August 14th to August 19th. Four days earlier (and mark that), as Ruth Loyd Miller brings out in her telling work, *Oaths Foresworn* in *"Love's Labour's Lost,"* (1990) the Queen had issued an edict forbidding "all resort of women to the lodgings of Cathedrals or Colleges." Of course it was just such an edict by the King of Navarre that provides the springboard for the action in Shakespeare's play; and when Biron asks, "Hath this been proclaimed?" Longaville replies, "Four days ago."

Two of young Edward's uncles had been poets, outstanding in their generation: Baron Sheffield and the well-known Earl of Surrey, who introduced blank verse and, with Sir Thomas Wyatt, the form of sonnet that came to be known as the Shakespearean after de Vere had been writing in it himself. In later years, as the Earl of Oxford, de Vere would receive a dedication as one "whose infancy from the beginning was ever sacred to the muses"; and I am emboldened to embrace the proposition that *The Tragical History of Romeus and Juliet,* a "childish" poem as Marchette Chute terms it, one derived from an Italian romance and clearly the basis of Shakespeare's play, was the work of the 12-year-old Edward, composed in the aftermath of Elizabeth's visit. The poem was published, in 1562, as by Arthur Brooke, it is true, but Brooke seems to be known for little else than drowning the next year; and George Turberville, who recorded the event, described the author of *The Tragical History* as a "dainty Babe" who on "Pallas' dug . . . did chew."

It was when Edward was 12 that his father died. The report that his mother remarried only three months later brings to mind Hamlet's bitterly reproaching the Queen his mother on her hasty remarriage; "Oh, God! a beast that wants discourse of reason/ Would have waited longer." This may have entered into a later idealization of his honored father as the old King Hamlet. Certainly when we read that Lord Robert Dudley, later the Earl of Leicester and the nearest to a husband Elizabeth was ever to have, received custody of the very extensive lands left by the 16th Earl, our identification of Leicester as Claudius will be re-inforced.

On his father's death, Edward was taken from his mother to become a royal ward, surely leading to the exchange in the opening of *All's Well that Ends Well:*

COUNTESS: In delivering my son from me I bury a second husband.
BERTRAM: And I, in going, madam, weep o'r my father's death

anew: but I must attend his majesty's command, to whom I am now in ward, evermore in subjection.

As a royal ward, Edward came under the guardianship of William Cecil, later Baron of Burghley. Cecil House, on the Strand, had grounds probably acres in extent, giving scope to the "greatest delight" its owner took "in making gardens, fountains and walks." For 20 years Cecil employed the most noted English horticulturalist of the time, John Gerard. (In 1977, *Horticulture* magazine, with a bow to believers in the Earl of Oxford as Shakespeare, noted the similarity between the last song in *Love's Labour's* and a passage in Gerard's *Herbal, or General History of Plants of 1597.*)

William Cecil Lord Burghley would be for 40 years Elizabeth's most trusted advisor. As a member of his household from the age of 12, close to the nexus of political power, Edward could have conceived "the relish and verve with which Shakespeare's characters speak the language of ambition, intrigue, and policy," to quote the veteran member of the Commons, Enoch Powell, who adds that "this authentic knowledge of how men think and act at the summit of political power . . . could only have been drawn from experience of the political struggle." In the domicile of Sir William and Lady Mildred, aunt of Francis Bacon and accounted one of the most learned women in the country, intellectual standards were undoubtedly high. Young Edward underwent a rigorous program of training and education, beginning daily at 7:00 a.m. with dancing, proceeding through French, Latin, writing and drawing, cosmography, more Latin and French and exercises with the pen. The tutor engaged for him, Lawrence Nowell, Dean of Litchfield, wrote to Sir William in 1563 that "my work for the Earl of Oxford cannot much longer be required." The next year the youth received his degree at St. John's College in ceremonies presided over by the Queen. Two months earlier, his maternal uncle, the scholar and translator Arthur Golding, had dedicated to him a learned work on Trogus Pompeus remarking on "how earnest a desire your honour hath naturally grafted in you to read, peruse and communicate with others as well the history of ancient times, and things done long ago, also the present state of things in our day, and not without a certain pregnancy of wit and ripeness of understanding": no small tribute to a 14-year-old.

Golding, dating the dedication from Cecil House and now undoubtedly Edward's tutor, had stronger reason yet to see in the youngster something like a future Shakespeare. There was then in preparation the only work for which Golding is remembered today, a translation of Ovid's *Metamorphoses*. The influence of the work on Shakespeare was such, as the militant orthodox scholar A.L. Rowse reminds us, that his contemporaries "spoke of him as an English Ovid." That Golding, a staunch and sober Puritan, should have undertaken to translate into English heptameters the 12,000-line work of a poet whose salacity contributed to his exile from Rome (no less) has astonished all commentators, while the racy, slangy, impish language of the translation is simply impossible to reconcile with Golding's other work, such as his translation of *John Calvin's version of the Psalms of David*. This, by the way, he also, in 1571, dedicated to his erstwhile charge, admonishing him that the word of God "is the light of your steps. Whosoever walketh without it walketh but in darkness, though he . . . had otherwise all the sciences, arts, cunning, eloquence, and wisdom of the world." Here is the kind of language we find if we dip into the supposed "collaboration" between Ovid and Golding, as where the goddess of agriculture is served an unappetizing "Hotchpotch":

> While Ceres was eating this, before hir gazing stood
> A hard-faced boy, a shrewd pert wag that could no manners good:
> He laughed at hir and in scorn did call hir "Greedie gut,"
> The Goddess being wroth therewith, did in the Hotchpotch put
> The liquor ere that all was eate, and in his face it threw. . . .

We may imagine the excitement when our literary mentors can no longer fail to recognize that THE XV BOOKES OF P. OVIDIUS NASO, ENTYTLED *Metamorphoses*, as published in installments in 1565 and 1567, while certainly composed under his uncle Arthur's tutelage, can only have been substantially the work of the boyish "Shakespeare." "The most beautiful book in the language," the poet Ezra Pound called it.

At 14, in ceremonies presided over by the Queen, Edward received a bachelor's degree from St. John's College, Oxford, where he had lodged for a spell. There, too, at 16, he was accorded a degree of Master of Arts. The next year, in 1567, he was enrolled at Gray's Inn, one of the Inns of Court which served, and still do, as law schools. Moreover, we read that in Gray's Inn especially the students "learned to dance, sing and play musical instruments" and performed "'masques' and 'revels.'" We know from Burghley's accounts that the young Earl at 19 was investing heavily in books. Among the classical texts were Plutarch's *Lives* (in French), always recognized as an essential part of Shakespeare's reading, and Chaucer, one of the sources of *Troilus and Cressida* (for the love-story). Of particular significance was his purchase of the Geneva Bible, for his copy of the book, bearing his heraldic device, was to be obtained by the Folger Shakespeare Library in Washington in 1925 and put on display in 1990. There it was closely examined by Roger Stritmatter who published a report on the many parallels, far beyond mere coincidence to account for, he found between passages marked in the Bible and passages in Shakespeare. (In a subsequent article on Oxford as Shakespeare by Walter Klier, a German periodical headed the section summarizing Stritmatter's report *Das Missing-link*.)

The youngster must not, however, be thought of as solely "bookish." For the first four years of his wardship, "the apparel, with rapier and daggers, for my Lord of Oxenford, his person," cost £627, an amount that would cover the total living costs of most of us for an equal period. The suspicion grows on the investigator, however, that Cecil took a substantial cut in his outlays for his ward. It is germane to note here the report of his biographer, . G.P.V. Akrigg, that the Earl of Southampton, as Cecil's ward, had to pay his guardian the "staggering sum" of £5000 for refusing to marry the girl chosen for him, an amount that, invested wisely today, would support one comfortably for life.

Oxford had imparted to Cecil his desire to "be called to the services of my Prince and country" and to see "the wars and services in strange and foreign lands." He was just short of his 20th birthday when his guardian yielded to his entreaties and he joined the Earl of Sussex in his campaign against the Scots. Much in Shakespeare must have been born in his experience of war on the border, his commander's siege of Hume Castle in particular perhaps standing him in good stead when Henry V laid siege to Harfleur. If young Faulconbridge and Bertram were born of that time, we can visualize them when Oxford entered a tournament at Westminster at 21. Another Cambridge man would write of him that:

> he controls his foaming steed with a light rein, and armed with a spear rides to the encounter. Fearlessly he settles himself in the saddle, gracefully bending his body this way and that. Now he circles round; now with spurred heels he touches his charger. The gallant animal [responds] with fiery energy . . . and again is pulled up short.
> Bravo, valiant youth!

Riding against the leading jousters of the day (including the Queen's own champion), Oxford, to the general amazement, won the "chief honour," a tablet of diamonds presented by Elizabeth. In the other two tournaments we know of his entering, he also copped first prize. Following that of 1571, one of the defendants in the contest wrote: "There is no man of life and agility in every respect in the Court but the Earl of Oxford."

His Marriage

Two months later, in July of 1571, another correspondent would write to the Earl of Rutland, a fellow ward of de Vere's: "The Earl of Oxford hath gotten him a wife—or a wife hath gotten him; this is Mistress Anne Cecil." Anne was 14, just a year older than Juliet. Her father had earlier in the year been made Baron Burghley, facilitating a match between an erstwhile commoner's daughter and the premier earl of the land. The match, which would prove the single greatest misfortune in the lives of all three, joined in lasting, close relationship two utterly unlike men, one aristocratic, mercurial, poetical and contemptuous of money, the other a self-made member of the new middle class, materialistic, crafty, hard-working, a devoted public servant—two men who outshone all their contemporaries in their respective fields, if we may trust the path that led us to the Earl of Oxford as Shakespeare. The plight of Anne, seeking to be loyal to both, was as that of Ophelia in just such circumstances.

Burghley would have preferred a match between his daughter and Philip Sydney, the powerful Earl of Leicester's nephew, "whom always I loved and esteemed," but the two had no relish for each other. This is made clear in the outspoken *Merry Wives of Windsor*, unmistakably an early play of the dramatist's given final touches around 1592. In this Sydney appears as Slender, of whom Anne Page remarks "what a world of ill-favored faults/ Looks handsome in three hundred pounds a year." (Sydney, who already had 80 pounds a year, was to receive 266 more from his uncle on his marriage to Anne Cecil.) The play was evidently designed by Oxford as a reassuring compliment to Anne. In it the young lord representing him revealingly declares to Anne that her father holds against him his "great birth," his indebtedness, his "riots past" and "wild societies" and further charges that "I should love thee but as a property." Upon Anne's observing "Maybe he tells you true," he confesses that her "father's wealth" was "the first motive that I woo'd thee" but protests that "'tis the very riches of thy self/ That now I aim at." In *All's Well that Ends Well* we are given a somewhat different angle on the match. In this it is Helena who speaks as Anne in exclaiming:

> That I should love a bright particular star
> And think to wed it, he is so above me.

(Hamlet "is a prince out of thy star," Polonius warns Ophelia.) However, Helena is elevated in rank, as Cecil was, to facilitate her marriage with Bertram, whom we remember taking leave of his mother, the Countess, to become a royal ward (a countess being the wife of an earl, of course). One judges that Elizabeth promoted the marriage of Oxford and Anne, as the monarch does their equivalents in the play, for Bertram cries:

> My wife, my liege! I shall beseech your highness
> in such a business give me leave to use
> The help of mine own eyes.

Oxford and Anne Cecil were married before the Queen on Christmas day 1571.

The Young Writer

Two weeks later Oxford contributed a 1,100-word preface in Latin to a translation into Latin by his former tutor at Cambridge of Baldassare Castiglione's *Il Cortegiano*. *The Courtier*, purported to be a discussion at the Court of the Duke of Urbino, "confessedly the purest and most elevated in Italy," on the question of what constituted the perfect courtier. The preface, which Gabriel Harvey would call more polished than the writings of Castiglione himself, was an astonishing piece of work for one who would be a junior in college today. In it, commending the translator for dedicating the work to his Queen, Oxford acclaimed Elizabeth as one "to whom alone is due all the praise of the Muses and *all the glory of literature*"—a phrase I think warrants italicizing. "The ideal of courtier, scholar, soldier," Drayton Henderson would write in the Everyman edition of the work, "perfected in the narrative of

Il Cortegiano, was Castiglione's gift to the world," and "Hamlet is the high exemplar of it in our literature." Henderson went on to declare with uncommon perception that "it is not only Shakespeare's Hamlet that seems to follow Castiglione; Shakespeare himself does."

The next year there was published Thomas Bedingfield's translation from the Latin of Girolamo Cardano's *De Consolatione*, the title page reading: "CARDANOS/ Comforte, translated/ And Published/ by commandment of the right/ Honorable the Earle of/ Oxenforde." The book commenced with a poem addressed to the Reader, its authorship openly and daringly acknowledged by the now 22-year-old nobleman, of which the first stanza reads:

> The laboring man that tills the fertile soil,
>   And reaps the harvest fruit, hath not indeed
> The gain but pain; but for all his toil
> He gets the straw, the lord will have the seed.

A strange complaint for a lord to make, unless he already foresaw being denied recognition of his toil, it was followed by a 770-word letter addressed "To my loving Friend Thomas Bedingfield, Esquire," and signed "From your loving and assured friend E. Oxenford." In the letter Oxford declared that the translation "shall comfort the afflicted, confirm the doubtful, encourage the coward, and lift up the baseminded, . . . whereto ought only the noble thoughts of men be inclined."

Macaulay would write of de Vere that "he shone at the Court of Elizabeth and won for himself an honourable place among the early masters of English poetry." E.K. Chambers, the great Elizabethan scholar, commenting on the dearth of distinguished poets in the generation following Wyatt and Surrey, declares that "The most hopeful of them was Edward de Vere, Earl of Oxford, a real courtier but an ill-conditioned youth, who became mute in later life." Mute *only* as Edward de Vere, we suggest. Whatever Chambers thought he meant by "ill-conditioned," an observer of the Court wrote when Oxford was 21, "the Queen delighteth more in his personage and his dancing and his valiantness than any other."

We shall return to that, but meanwhile there is the quality of de Vere's verse to consider. Stratfordians make a great issue of its inferiority to that of Shakespeare's. In fact, his verse sounds much as one would expect a youthful Shakespeare's to sound (in contrast to

the youthful verse of the orthodox "Shakespeare," which—to repeat—has never been heard of). Take the sestet of a sonnet by de
Vere and one by Shakespeare, and unless we recognize either,
could we be sure whose is whose?

> In constant truth to bide so firm and sure,
> To scorn the world regarding but thy friends?
> With patient mind each passion to endure,
> In one desire to settle to the end?
> Love then thy choice where such choice thou bind,
> As nought but death shall ever change thy mind.
>
> What merit do I in myself respect,
> That is so proud thy service to despise,
> When all my best doth worship thy defect,
> Commanded by the motion of thine eyes:
> But love hate on, for now I know my mind;
> Those that can see thou lov'st, and I am blind.

Some years ago, the late Professor Louis B. Bénézet of
Dartmouth College made up an amalgam of verse attributed respectively to the Earl of Oxford and to Shakespeare consisting of
about 35 lines of each, no passage longer than eight lines or shorter
than four. It follows—and I may say that I know of no one who has
been able to say without cribbing which selections are whose:

> If care of skill could conquer vain desire,
> Or reason's reins my strong affections stay:
> There should my sighs to quiet breast retire,
> And shun such sights as secret thoughts betray;
> Uncomely love, which now lurks in my breast
> Should cease, my grief by wisdom's power oppressed.
> My reason, the physician to my love,
> Angry that his prescriptions are not kept,
> Hath left me, and I desperate now approve
> Desire is death, which physic did except.
> Past cure I am, now reason is past care,
> And frantic mad with evermore unrest.
> Fain would I sing but fury makes me fret,
> And rage hath sworn to seek revenge of wrong;
> My mazed mind in malice is so set,
> As death shall daunt my deadly dolours long;

Patience perforce is such a pinching pain,
As die I will or suffer wrong again.
For if I should despair, I should go mad,
And in my madness might speak ill of thee:
Now this ill-wresting world is grown so bad,
Mad slanderers by mad ears believed be.
Love is a discord and a strange divorce
Betwixt our sense and rest, by whose power,
As mad with reason, we admit that force
Which wit or labour never may endower.
My thoughts and my discourse as madmen's are,
As random from the truth vainly express'd;
For I have sworn thee fair and thought thee bright
Who art as black as hell and dark as night.
Why should my heart think that a several plot
Which my heart knows the wide world's common place?
Or mine eyes seeing this, say this is not,
To put fair truth upon so foul a face?
Who taught thee first to sigh, alas, my heart?
Who taught thy tongue the woeful words of plaint?
Who filled your eyes with tears of bitter smart?
Who gave thee grief and made thy joys to faint?
Who first did paint with colours pale thy face?
Who first did break thy sleeps of quiet rest?
Above the rest in court who gave thee grace?
Who made thee strive in honour to be best?
Who taught thee how to make me love thee more
The more I hear and see just cause of hate?
O, though I love what others do abhor,
With others thou shouldst not abhor my state:
What worldly wight can hope for heavenly hire,
When only signs must make his secret moan:
A silent suit doth seld to grace aspire,
My hapless hap doth roll the restless stone.
Yet Phoebe fair disdained the heavens above,
To 'joy on earth her poor Endymion's love.
And shall I live on earth to be her thrall?
And shall I live and serve her all in vain?
And shall I kiss the steps that she lets fall?
And shall I pray the gods to keep the pain
From her that is so cruel still?
No, no, on her work all your will.

And let her feel the power of all your might,
And let her have her most desire with speed,
And let her pine away both day and night,
And let her moan and none lament her need;
And let all those that shall her see,
Despise her state and pity me.
Let him have time to tear his curled hair,
Let him have time against himself to rave
Let him have time of Time's help to despair,
Let him have time a beggar's orts to crave,
And time to see one that by alms doth live
Disdain to him disdained scraps to give.

Oxford and Elizabeth

In a passage quoted by Mr. Justice John Paul Stevens in his
illuminating comparison of the cases for Shakspere of Stratford and
the Earl of Oxford, Carolly Erickson writes in *The First Elizabeth*
(1983) that the Queen,

it was said, was seducing handsome young men and keeping them
under surveillance by her well-paid spies. . . . Prominent among these
favorites was Edward de Vere, earl of Oxford, a boyish, hazel-eyed
young courtier [who] excelled at the courtly graces Elizabeth admired.
He was athletic and acquitted himself brilliantly in the tilt-yard. . . .
He was an agile and energetic dancer, the ideal partner for the Queen,
and had a refined ear for music and was a dexterous performer on the
virginals. His poetry was unmistakably accomplished, and his education
had given him a cultivated mind, at home with the antique authors
Elizabeth knew so well.

That Elizabeth and Oxford were lovers can scarcely be
doubted. It is, for one thing, virtually the only inference to be
drawn from an anonymous and astonishing publication that appeared in September 1594 and made the first known reference to
Shakespeare by name apart from the dedications of the two long
narrative poems. This came in an introductory couplet reading:

Yet Tarquin plucks his glistering grape,
And Shake-speare paints poor Lucrece rape.

Willobie His Avisa, composed of hundreds of fast-paced, professional stanzas, tells the story of Avisa's suitors, whose initials, as Professor G.B. Harrison writes, "concealed, or rather revealed to contemporaries, persons of great importance; so great, in fact, that the scandals about them were still commercially worth retailing 40 years later," despite its inclusion in 1599 "in the category of books to be burned." *Avisa* unquestionably represents Queen Elizabeth. She signs herself ALWAYS THE SAME AVISA, which, translated into Latin, as Professor G.P.V. Akrigg observes, becomes the motto of Elizabeth, *Semper Eadem*.

Another Canadian professor, Barbara N. DeLuna, of the University of Alberta, cites half a dozen attributes of Avisa shared by Elizabeth. In one episode, "H.W.," "at length not able any longer to endure the burning heat" of his passion for "A," decides to seek the counsel of "his familiar friend," "W.S." That "H.W." is described as young reinforces the general consensus that he stands for Henry Wriothesley, Earl of Southampton, then 21. However, as Professor DeLuna points out, he is evidently to be identified with the alleged author of the *roman à clef*, Henrico Willobego, and probably compounds Southampton with his close associate, Robert Devereux, Earl of Essex, Elizabeth's last light of love. That "W.S." stands for William Shakespeare is recognized by scholars from John Payne Collier to E.K. Chambers and Samuel Schoenbaum. The implications are seismic. W.S. advises "friend Harry" how to prevail with Avisa. "Apply her still with divers things. . . Sometimes with gold, sometimes with rings." He must admire "her wisdom and her virtuous ways";

> Say 'twas her wit and modest show
> That made you like and love her so.

W.S. draws on his own experience in continuing:

> Well, say no more; I know thy grief,
> And face from whence these flames arise.
> It is not hard to find relief,
> If thou wilt follow good advice:
>   She is no Saint, She is no Nun;
>   I think in time she may be won.

What the professoriat would have us believe is that the proud, sought-after Earl of Southampton would make a "familiar friend" of a common player of Shakspere's origins, submit to being called "friend Harry" by him and solicit his advice on how to win the amorous favors of the Queen of England, the matrimonial prize of the Western world. Far more even than that, academe would have it that the "upstart Crow" (as the professoriat would have us believe Robert Greene termed Shakspere) would presume to pronounce Elizabeth neither Saint nor Nun and had himself—yes *himself*—tried "like assaults" on her virtue and obtained the "relief" he sought! I think it may be stated as a matter of simple fact that, all things considered, the only possible William Shakespeare was Edward de Vere, the 17th Earl of Oxford. Even so, we must be amazed that *Willobie His Avisa* ever survived the sale of its first copy.

The testimony of *Willobie* comports with other evidence that Elizabeth and Oxford were lovers. This includes certain of Shakespeare's *Sonnets*, the innuendos of *Venus and Adonis*, and the only interpretation, I believe, to be drawn from the love between Sylvia and Valentine in *Two Gentlemen of Verona* (which may well be seen as meaning two gentlemen of one Vere). The story, in its far-reaching dimensions, is beyond exploring here. But this much we may say. There were compelling reasons why the authorship of Shakespeare's works had to be dissimulated. The premier earl of England could not be seen writing for the common theatre (let alone sneaking on the stage himself) and consorting with actors (doubtless the "lewd friends" Burghley held against his son-in-law); and Oxford's name would carry over to Burghley's grandchildren. The identification of the dramatist as a member of the inner circle of the Court would expose the highly-placed, real-life originals of outstanding characters in the plays for who they were. But even more decisive was the awareness that those plays, and the poems as well, if read as of Oxford's authorship must open the public's eyes to his relations with Elizabeth and its consequences; and this, it is clear, the Court meant at all costs to prevent. What a story it is!—and one to which only Shakespeare could do justice, as he did, so far as he dared. And he dared a great deal.

"This Is I, Hamlet the Dane!"

We may say that the principals of *Hamlet* have in the main now taken their places on stage. That the Prince is the dramatist revealing himself seems, again, unmistakable, with the complication that he is virtually a college-boy at the start and, after the supposed lapse of only a few months, nearing middle age by the play's end. Polonius has, of course, long been recognized as an irreverent rendition of Burghley; even E.K. Chambers asks if "Polonius can have resembled some nickname of Burghley" (which it did, Polus) and says that "Laertes is less like Robert Cecil than Burghley's elder son Thomas." (As Chambers cannot have failed to be aware, anyone other than a courtier enjoying the protection of the Queen who had mocked the powerful Burghley on the stage would have been clapped into the Fleet and every copy of the play have been destroyed. In the first version of *Hamlet*, moreover, the dramatist played brazenly on Burghley's motto, *Cor unum*, and called Polonius Corambis—double hearted.) To see Elizabeth in Gertrude takes no great imagination; but here we come to an interesting ambivalence in Hamlet's attitude toward her. Gertrude is Hamlet's mother, as, in a sense, Elizabeth was also Oxford's as his queen and one old enough to have been his mother. However, Elizabeth was also his lover, and beginning with John Barrymore (I am told), actors playing Hamlet have interpreted his feeling for Gertrude as to a degree incestuous.

As Gertrude is Elizabeth, so Claudius is conspicuously Robert Dudley, Earl of Leicester. A "lecherous villain" in more eyes than Oxford's, he was the nearest to a husband Elizabeth ever had, and if he did not murder an earlier mate of hers to win his position, he was widely believed to have murdered his own to do so. Scandal, moreover, made him the poisoner of the noble Earl of Sussex, to whom de Vere seems to have stood in a somewhat filial relationship after the Scottish campaign. Significantly, as we have seen, Leicester won custody of the boy Edward's inheritance, the Oxford estates, upon his father's death.

That leaves Horatio, of whom we are told in Hamlet's loving address:

> A man that Fortune's buffets and rewards
> Hast ta'en with equal thanks; and blest are those
> Whose blood and judgment are so well commingled
> That they are not a pipe for Fortune's finger
> To sound what stop she please.

Oxford had two cousins, Francis and Horace Vere, illustrious military captains, of whom G.M. Trevelyan writes that the English forces in the Netherlands, "led by 'the fighting Veres' helped to defeat . . . the infantry of Spain, till then unconquerable in the open field." Revealingly, a report has come down to us of Horace that "it was true of him what is said of the Caspian Sea, that it doth never ebb nor flow, observing a constant tenor, neither elated nor depressed." (Horace would share with his elder brother the imposing tomb erected to Francis Vere in Westminster Abbey. It is possible that Edward de Vere would be interred there too, without fanfare or public record, for another first cousin, Arthur Golding's son, would write of him that "I will only speak what all men's voices confirm: he was a man in mind and body absolutely accomplished with honorable endowments; he died at his house in Hackney in the month of June Anno 1604 and lieth buried at Westminster.")

"I Was Then A Young Traveler"

At 23, Oxford, presumably suffering from the stultification of Court life, took part in some rare highjinks, a mock hold-up of two former employees at Gad's Hill on the highway between Gravesend and Rochester, in exactly the place where Prince Hal with his companions of the Boar's Head would engage in just such an escapade in *Henry the Fourth, Part One*. Seven months later, in January 1573, he would be guilty of a much graver infraction, stealing away to the continent without royal consent, the Queen sending his friend Thomas Bedingfield after him to bring him back. A year later, having wrung from Elizabeth and Burghley their reluctant consent, and now 24, he set off again for the continent, with a small retinue.

The Louvre was then under construction and it was at Blois, probably, that Oxford was presented to the king, Henry III, and his queen, the former remarking, upon learning that the young man was married, "There, then, is a *beau couple*." With the earl ready to depart, the Venetian ambassador wrote a report to Burghley on his conduct ("as might be desired" and "without the likelihood of any other") recalling Polonius's having had a spy put on his son Laertes in Paris to observe him and even to provoke scandal about him. In mid March also came news from his father-in-law to make Oxford "a glad man," as he wrote in reply, and to "thank God" that Lady Anne was with child. At the same time he stressed in his letter, as he would repeatedly, his need of funds.

On leaving Paris, Oxford went far out of his way, with a reduced retinue, to visit Johannes Sturm—Sturmius—the influential German scholar, with whom he remained until late April. Sturm was then 70, and the year before his death, with the Protestant North in dire peril from the Spanish legions, he would appeal for an English commander to lead its defense, Oxford being his first choice.

In Italy, Oxford headed for a city famous for its university, where he could exclaim with Lucentio in *The Taming of the Shrew* that he was

> . . . To Padua come, as he that leaves
> A shallow plash to plunge him in the deep,
> And with satiety seeks to quench his thirst.

From Padua, in due course, Oxford and his party traveled to Genoa, having a chance to behold

> . . . the Alps and Apennines,
> The Pyrenean and the River Po.

In late September Oxford wrote his father-in-law of his "return now to Venice" and of his recovery from a fever. He also reported that "By reason of my great charges of travel and sickness have taken up of Master Baptista Negrone 500 crowns, which I shall desire your Lordship to see them repaid." Later we learn of his having a remittance from a Pasquino Spinola, and in the two names we are brought very close to the Baptista Minola whose "crowns" are repeatedly mentioned by Petruchio in *The Taming of the Shrew*, which is laid in Padua. In the letter speaking of his indebtedness to Negrone, Oxford writes of "hoping by this time my money which is made of the sale of my land is all come in." This is a recurrent theme of his relations with Burghley, bringing to mind *As You Like It* and Rosalind's exclaiming to Jaques, in whom we may see the melancholy side of the dramatist, "I fear you have sold your own lands to see other men's; then to have seen much and to have nothing is to have rich eyes and poor hands."

On December 12th, the young earl left Padua for Florence, whence, three weeks later, he set off for Siena. In *All's Well* we hear the King of France tell his restless young courtiers:

> The Florentines and Senoys are by the ears; . . .
> Yet, for our gentlemen that mean to see
> The Tuscan service, freely have they leave
> To stand on either part.

The chivalric view would have come naturally to Oxford: what mattered was not which side you were on but how you fought.

Addressing Burghley again from Siena, he would anticipate Antonio's confession in *The Merchant of Venice* that "my creditors grow cruel, my estate is very low." He wrote that "My Lord, I am sorry to hear how hard my fortune is in England" and went on to speak of "the greatness of my debt and greediness of my creditors." As for such benefits as might come to him, "my son must give the thanks." Near the end of the long letter he would complain that "I am to content myself according to the English proverb that it is my hap to starve while the grass doth grow." In *Hamlet*, when Rosencrantz reminds him of the advancement that will be his in time, the young prince replies: "Ay, Sir, but 'while the grass grows'—the proverb is something musty."

His letters to his father-in-law notwithstanding, the 24-year-old must have been enjoying himself to have brooked royal displeasure (as evidently he did) by protracting his stay in Italy. There, according to report, he bought a house, in Venice, setting a precedent for future generations of his countrymen. He must have entered very much into the fun, so to speak, for in a book published in Naples in 1699 (and discovered by Julia Cooley Altrochi in 1969) he figures in the mock "Tirade of the Tournament" as recited by Graziano, a stock character of the *Commedia dell' Arte*. Before various crowned heads and other worthies, Elmund, Milord of Oxford, jousts with Alvida, Countess of Edenburg, both contestants ending sprawled in the dust! The Emperor Polidor awards gifts from antiquity to all the knights and amazons, Milord of Oxford receiving the magic horn of the paladin of Charlemagne to rout armies and a spear of sorts to shake, with enchanted consequences. Graziano, we are reminded in the Arden Shakespeare, finds his counterpart in Holofernes in *Love's Labour's Lost*. Throughout that play, we may recall, Professor Kittredge found the influence of the *Commedia dell 'Arte*, of which, we need not doubt, Oxford was an enthusiastic patron.

We may be altogether certain that he would not have forgone a pilgrimage to Rome and the monuments of Julius Caesar's time and have seen upon a "gusty day / The troubled Tiber chafing with her shores." Shipping for Sicily, he would have put in at Naples; "I'll bring you to your ship and so to Naples," Prospero will promise its King and that "noble Neapolitan, Gonzalo." Noting the nasal twang of the townsfolk (if we may trust reports), the dramatist would have the Clown in *Othello* declare, "Why, masters, have your instruments been in Naples, that they speak i' th' nose thus?"

In Palermo, an English army officer would report,

The Right Honourable the Earl of Oxford, a famous man of chivalry, . . . made a challenge against all manner of persons whatsoever, . . . with horse and armour, to fight a combat with him in defense of his Prince and Country. For which he was very highly commended, and yet no man be so hardy to encounter with him.

In crossing the straits between the toe of the boot of Italy and Sicily Oxford would have passed the Lipari Islands, in which, as Richard P. Roe has pointed out, Prospero and his fellows, their ship beset by a northwester, could have been expected to seek shelter. The Liparis are volcanic (Stromboli is among them) as the island in *The Tempest* explicitly is and as Bermuda is not. And here may be the place to scotch the notion that it was in Bermuda that the voyagers in the play sought refuge in sailing from Tunis to Naples. This is of course absurd and is based simply on Prospero's having called up his familiar spirit, Ariel, from "the still-vexed Bermoothes," of the vexed nature of which Oxford had reason to know.

Oxford's youth would have made him the more susceptible to things Italian, and for these he would later be mocked in a fit of spleen by Gabriel Harvey in his *Speculum Tuscanismi*, the "Mirror of Tuscanism":

His cringing side neck, eyes glancing, fisnamic smirking,
With forefinger kiss, and brave embrace to the footward.
. . .
A little Apish hat couched fast to the pate like an oyster,
French Camarack ruffs, deep with a whiteness starched to
the purpose.
Every one A per se A, his terms and braveries in print,
Delicate in speech, quaint in array: conceited in all points,
In Courtly guiles a passing singular odd man,

and here Harvey's admiration breaks forth, putting posterity lastingly in his debt—

For Gallants a brave mirror, a Primrose of Honour,

A Diamond for nonce, a fellow peerless in England,
Not the like discourser for Tongue, and head to be found out,
Not the like resolute man for great and serious affairs,
Not the like Lynx to spy out secrets and privities of States,
Eyed like to Argus, . . . wing'd like to Mercury. . . .

Oxford would remain away from England for 15 months, probably taking ship from Italy "to Marseilles, to which place/ We have convenient convoy." In April he departed Paris for home. His ship crossing the Channel was captured by pirates, as Hamlet's would be en route to England; but, very likely, as in Hamlet's case he could report that "they dealt with me like thieves of mercy." Evidently they left him with the array of gifts he was bringing the Queen, including, as John Stow records in his famous *Annals*, "a pair of perfumed gloves," in which "the Queen took such pleasure . . . that she was pictured with those gloves upon her hand, and for many years after it was called the Earl of Oxford's perfume."

What the young nobleman brought back from his travels was, I think, not just the trappings of Italy but the spirit of the Renaissance. In the afterglow of the delight and stimulation we know he had found in Italy, which were to lead to Shakespeare's happiest plays, he was ill-prepared for news that would now bowl him over.

While in Venice he had welcomed the delayed word of his wife's having been delivered of a daughter. It would appear that by the time of his return to Paris at the end of March 1576 the Court was abuzz with speculation that the Countess of Oxford's child was not his. These tidings were divulged to the young husband in Paris by a "receiver" of his, Rowland Yorke, who later would defect to the Spanish and be poisoned by them to forestall a further betrayal. We know him, I should guess, for his contribution to Parolles in *All's Well*, a braggart captain and follower of Bertram's, on whom his baleful influence is exercised only when he is shown up as a coward and traitor.

A Marriage Sundered

The consequence of Yorke's report was that Oxford refused for five years to live with his wife.

What are we to make of this tragedy, which was to leave such an impress on our finest literature? While Oxford's letter to Burghley in 1572 pledged with almost Shakespearean eloquence his loyalty to and support of the Queen's first minister following the St. Bartholomew's Day massacre of the Protestants in France, relations between the two were bound to be strained by temperamental differences. Then, too, Oxford was hardly one to forgive the Burghleys' having him spied upon and seeking to subborn his servants. Without doubt, moreover, the marriage of Edward de Vere and Anne Cecil had been doomed to failure. Edward Dowden illuminates a major difficulty between them in speaking of "Hamlet, with his piteous, foiled love of one who can give him no help or understanding sympathy." Ophelia, we remember, sided with her father in the crunch, denying her knowledge that he is eavesdropping on them. "Receive her into your house," Oxford wrote his father-in-law on the report of Anne's infidelity, "for there, as your daughter or her mother's, more than my wife, you may take comfort of her."

But had Anne been unfaithful? Here we enter murky mystery that probably will never be resolved. It seems certainly to tell us something of the dramatist that in play after play a male protagonist, on the flimsiest grounds, comes to suspect a faithful mate of infidelity and to reject her callously and cruelly. This is true of Proteus's treatment of Julia in *Two Gentlemen*, of Angelo's of Mariana in *Measure for Measure*, of Bertram's of Helena in *All's Well*, of Claudio's of Hero in *Much Ado*. Indeed, in three plays the husband's vengeful animosity is actively murderous while the wives who incur it—Imogen in *Cymbeline*, Hermione in *The Winter's Tale* and Desdemona in *Othello*—are among the saintliest of Shakespeare's heroines. I am but one who cannot help seeing Oxford as self-accused in his dark side as the Moor, with Anne as Desdemona, who "was half the wooer," Burghley as Brabantio, in "effect a voice as potential . . . as the Duke's," and Rowland Yorke as Iago, "that Spartan dog."

So Oxford stands convicted in his own words as the indefensible and brutal condemner of an innocent wife? By no means necessarily. In March 1575, just two months to the day after Oxford departed England, the Queen's physician wrote Burghley a letter relating at length how his stricken daughter had confessed in misery that she stood in doubt whether her husband would "pass upon her and her unborn child." Burghley, too, two months later, in a confused note to himself, expressed fear that Edward would not accept the child as his. Later, after his son-in-law's return he would write retrospectively: "2nd July. The Countess delivered of a baby." Then: "24th September. The letter of the Earl giving thanks for his wife's delivery. Mark well this letter."

Does not the sequence of events demonstrate, then, that Anne had conceived a child not her husband's? Well, again, not necessarily. There are two extraordinary reports, seemingly valid, one that Oxford "forsook his lady's bed [but] the father of Lady Anne contrived that her husband should unknowingly sleep with her, believing her to be another woman, and she bore a son to him in consequence." The other has a daughter born of the "virtuous deceit." The question is, did this clandestine union of Edward and Anne actually take place, or was this what Edward was told to cover Anne's infidelity? In either case, of course, he would have had to be not quite himself "with the drinking of old sack"—to which there are no less than 45 references in Shakespeare's plays. Whatever the truth, it surely says a lot that the ruse of the switched ladies is employed in *All's Well* to bring Bertram to bed with his wife, Helena, to produce an heir, and in *Measure for Measure* to bring Angelo to consummate his marriage-by-pre-contract with Mariana. What may be significant is that in the first instance the lady of the tryst is called Diana, a conventional appellation for Elizabeth, and in the second Isabella, Spanish for Elizabeth.

So we now know how Oxford was brought back to Lady Anne in aching self-recrimination? Once more we cannot be sure. It may be that the ruse was extraneous and Oxford came to see Anne as more sinned against than sinning; but this takes us into waters too dark and deep for this limited excursion. Yet Othello's despairing cry must echo in our ears: "But yet the pity of it, Iago, O, Iago the pity of it, Iago!"

A Budding "Shakespeare"—and the Dark Lady

In 1576, the year of Oxford's return from the continent, construction of the first playhouse, the Theatre, was begun by James Burbage, father of Richard, while nearby another, the Curtain, would arise soon after. The next year saw a performance at Hampton Court of "The historie of Error," surely an early version of *The Comedy of Errors,* of which the "doggerel verse," as Edward Dowden calls it, marks it as one of the earliest of the Shakespearean plays (and one that aims a joke at a courtier inimical to Oxford, Christopher Hatton, who would be unmistakably mocked as Malvolio in *Twelfth Night*). Less than two months later, a play was shown at Whitehall registered as *The Hystorie of Titus and Gissi-*

pus, which we are probably safe in taking as a scribal error for *Titus Andronicus.* Two plays, incidentally, could scarcely be found to show the two masks of a dramatist in greater contrast than the near-slapstick of one and the brutal horror of the other.

In 1576, again, there was published *The Paradise of Daintie Devices,* a collection of poems, of which eight were signed E.O.— and for a living nobleman to identify himself as the author of published verse was a daring departure from convention. (In an anthology of 1872, Alexander B. Grosart would publish 22 poems he attributed to Oxford, of whom he made the perspicacious observation that "An unlifted shadow lies across his memory.") In these, it requires no great imagination to perceive an immature Shakespeare. Take the first stanza of *The Meeting with Desire:*

> The lively lark stretched forth her wing,
>   The messenger of Morning bright,
> And with her cheerful voice did sing,
>   The Day's approach, discharging Night;
> When that Aurora blushing red,
>   Descried the guilt of Thetis' bed.

When to this we add from another poem of Oxford's

> When Phoebus from the bed
> Of Thetis doth arise. . . .

we can hardly fail to be reminded of the song from *Cymbeline:*

> Hark, hark! the lark at Heaven's gate sings,
> And Phoebus gins arise

One must resist the temptation to multiply examples, noting only that five of E.O.'s poems in *Daintie Devices* are in the stanza-form of *Venus and Adonis.*

The position Oxford had achieved in letters by the age of 28 was recognized in an extraordinary address before the Queen by Gabriel Harvey, then a fellow at Trinity College, Cambridge. After eulogizing in turn the three most powerful personages in the realm—Elizabeth herself, Leicester and Burghley—Harvey turned to de Vere and, versifying in Latin as before, proclaimed:

Thy splendid fame, great Earl, demands even more than in the case of others the services of a poet possessing lofty eloquence. Thy merit doth not creep along the ground, nor can it be confined within the limits of a song.

Reading the peroration, I am persuaded that Oxford had put Harvey up to impelling the Queen to release him to win distinction in the wars, like his cousins, the "fighting Veres." To pick up a bit farther in Harvey's exhortation:

Do thou but go forward boldly. . . . Mars will obey thee, Hermes will be thy messenger, Pallas striking her shield with her spear shaft will attend thee. For a long time past Phoebus Apollo has cultivated thy mind in the arts. English poetical measures have been sung by thee long enough. Let the Courtly Epistle to the reader of *The Courtier*—more polished even than the writings of Castiglione himself—witness how greatly thou dost excel in letters. I have seen many Latin verses of thine, yea, even more English verses are extant; thou hast not only drunk deep draughts of the Muses of France and Italy, but thou has learned the manners of many men and the arts of foreign countries. . . . O thou hero worthy of renown, throw away the insignificant pen, throw away bloodless books; . . . Now is the time to sharpen the spear and handle great engines of war. . . . Now all martial influences support thy eager mind driving out the cares of peace. Pull Hannibal up short at the gates of Britain, defended though he be by a mighty host. Let Don John of Austria come on only to be driven home again. . . . In thy breast is noble blood. Courage animates thy brow, Mars lives in thy tongue, thine eyes flash fire, thy countenance shakes spears. . . . [The translation of the last two words is optional.]

It would, however, be some years before Elizabeth would yield to such entreaties.

Ten years after this, Oxford's brother-in-law would be adding military lustre to the family through his command of English forces on the continent. This is relevant here because it was in 1578 that Lady Mary Vere married the fetchingly named Peregrine Bertie, the future Lord Willoughby d'Eresby. Relations between the two proved to be troubled; Burghley's son Thomas wrote to his father of an "unkindness" that had grown up between the two and anticipated that Lady Mary "will be beaten with that rod which heretofore she prepared for others." It is difficult not to see in the couple the Katharina and Petrucio of *The Taming of the Shrew* and an early version of the play itself in *A Morall of the Marriage of Mynde and Measure*, which was enacted at Richmond (much favored by the Queen) in 1579. It is certain, anyway, that Lord Willoughby led a diplomatic mission to the Danish king at Elsinore—and, as television-producer John Mucci has pointed out, brought back guest lists from social functions containing the names Rosencrantz and Guildenstern.

"I am but mad north-northwest," Hamlet would avow—and with reason. It was at this time, in the late 1570s, that Oxford invested heavily in Martin Frobisher's unsuccessful search for a northwest passage around North America to Cathay. Others included the Queen and Burghley. The lodestone was not only the passage but gold. Appetites were whetted by the assay reports of 200 tons of ore that were brought back. A fleet was dispatched to bring back 2,000. Oxford put up £3,000, just as Antonio in *The Merchant of Venice* was in bond for 3,000 ducats. Unfortunately, the parallel did not stop there. Stock in the enterprise had been issued by one Michael Lok, a London merchant with a Mediterranean business, who was later sent to jail on the charge of falsifying the assay reports. With the prefix "Shy" (which Shakespeare used in the sense we do in "shyster"), his name would be infamous centuries later, though as the Jew he would be allowed to voice his case—the dramatist being what he was—in words no less immortal in their poignance. Oxford's loss was as enormous as Antonio's when "all his ventures failed," dashing his "hopes abroad."

The year 1580 was momentous for our story in bringing to Court the 20-year-old bewitching niece of the Knyvets, who held prominent positions among the Queen's attendants. Anne Vavasor was to cut quite a swath in life through her male acquaintances and to have three husbands, two at once, or so it would be alleged in 1618. A brunette of slim stature and narrow, perhaps calculating face, Anne was appointed Gentlewoman of the Bedchamber, and it cannot have been long before she and Oxford were in each other's arms. We meet her first, or I am much mistaken, as Rosaline of *Love's Labour's Lost*, which Ruth Loyd Miller persuades us was a reflection of the English Court between 1578 and 1583. Sir Sydney Lee observes that in his Sonnets 127 and 132, "Shakespeare amiably notices the black complexion, hair and eyes of his mistress" and "repeats almost verbatim his own lines in *Love's Labour's Lost* (iv iii, 241-247)." There can be little doubt, I think, that Anne Vavasor is known to us as the Dark Lady of the *Sonnets*.

In March 1581 Anne was delivered of a child, a boy, by Oxford and all three were committed to the Tower by the Queen; those who served England's Majesty served a jealous mistress, though Oxford's affair with her had doubtless long been over. Little Edward Vere, as he would be named, would grow up to attend the University of Leyden and would become a captain in the service of Sir Francis and Sir Horace Vere and be knighted. What his relations with his father would be is, however, today a total mystery.

One hopes that Elizabeth showed the young mother more lenience than she did Anne's paramour. Oxford remained imprisoned for two and a half months, it would appear, and would then be kept under house arrest. In his time in prison he may well have mulled over the circumstances he would dramatize in *King Richard the Third*, in which the Tower is mentioned 26 times. By depicting Richard in the most evil, sardonic hues, the dramatist reminds Elizabeth all the more forcefully of her indebtedness to the 13th Earl of Oxford, who played a leading role in bringing down Shakespeare's monster and establishing the Tudors on the throne. I should guess that the immediately preceding play, *King Henry the Sixth, Part Three*, in which the same Earl is continually acclaimed, was written at this time. The anonymous play, *The Famous Victories of Henry the Fift*, [sic] from which the two-part *King Henry the Fourth* and *King Henry the Fifth* were indisputably to evolve, had, we may judge, been written by Oxford a good deal earlier. In it the 11th Earl of Oxford plays a central role, even beyond historical warrant, especially at the battle of Agincourt. In this play, too, the mock hold-up staged at Gad's Hill by Prince Hal is first enacted, faithful to the one staged by the young Edward de Vere.

These were bleak times for Edward, now entering upon his 30s. His affair with Anne Vavasor cannot have been cheap for a lover to whom second thoughts about expenditures were better left to tradesmen. His support of fellow writers went beyond that of any other patron. We read of his making a New Year's day gift to Elizabeth of "a fair jewel of gold, being a ship garnished fully with diamonds and a mean pearl pendant." We are taken to the lavish establishment maintained by Timon of Athens. Oxford had authorized his father-in-law "to sell any portion of my land." "Let all my land be sold," Timon grandly proclaims when all his is gone. Between 1576 and 1584, 47 sales of Oxford's properties are recorded. In addition to his other expenses, Oxford had taken over the Earl of Warwick's company of players early in 1580 and would maintain one or two troupes for the rest of his life. The two precedent earls were both known for their acting companies, which would tour the country in the summer and for the rest of the year be available at Castle Hedingham. ("Shakespeare," Dr. John Ward would report, "frequented the plays all his younger time.") It is startling to read how in the summer of 1580, Burghley wrote to the Chancellor of Oxford University to "commend . . . my Lord of Oxford his players, that they might show their cunning in certain plays already performed by them before the Queen's Majesty."

"Against A Sea of Troubles"

That same year, 1580, the year before Anne Vavasor gave birth to his child, brought a crisis in Oxford's life and the heaping of a lasting slander on his name. Shakespeare's fondness for friars cannot escape notice, and though the plays testify to their author's pervasive skepticism, a leaning toward Roman Catholicism has been observed in them. The solemn and gorgeous bastion of historical continuity and hierarchy, the Church of Rome had evidently struck a responsive chord in the young de Vere in Italy. Fifteen Earls of Oxford had been christened, married and buried in the old faith. "A backward-looking man," A.L. Rowse has said of Shakespeare, "with a dream of an older England at heart," while Walt Whitman saw the historical plays as "conceived out of the fullest heat and pulse of feudalism." Soon after his return from Italy, it was reported that Oxford and several of his friends, including Lord Henry Howard, Charles Arundel and Francis Southwell, had made a secret profession of adherence to the Roman Catholic religion. At the end of *Cymbeline*, the British king proclaims that "we submit to Caesar/ And to the Roman Empire," with the proviso that "A Roman and a British ensign wave/ Friendly together." But this is after the Britons have defeated an invading Roman legion.

In 1580 there was another kind of invasion from Rome, "the Jesuit invasion." A hundred of their order, trained by a fanatical English monk and a pope who had had a medal struck commemorating the massacre of St. Bartholomew, came to England, no doubt, as they gave out, to bring instruction to adherents of the Old Religion. But to the Protestant half of the population, loyalty to that religion meant disloyalty to England. Moreover, it was at this time that the "Spanish Fury" under the Duke of Parma was raging against the Protestants in the Low Countries with consequences "overlaying even the memory of St. Bartholomew," Elizabeth

Jenkins writes. The garrison of Maestricht was "slaughtered with maniacal fury, . . . the women who manned its defenses torn to pieces," and every Englishman knew "that when King Philip had reduced the Netherlands to his will, England's turn would come next."

Like someone else we know, Posthumus in *Cymbeline*, had journeyed to Rome, also to return an "Italianate Englishman," as it were, declaring:

> I am brought thither
> Among the Italian gentry, and to fight
> Against my lady's kingdom. . . .

Addressing his native Britain, he vows "I'll give no wound to thee," and

> so I'll fight
> Against the part I come with. . . .

So it would be with Oxford. He divulged his reasons for suspecting the loyalty of his three associates in the alleged pledge of allegiance to Roman Catholicism—suspicions that would be amply borne out in the case of two. The flavor of the episode may perhaps be imparted by the unmasking of the three traitors by Henry V aboard the ship preparing to depart for France. Henry Howard, conniving with Mary Queen of Scots, would prove to be an inveterate traitor to his friends, including the Earl of Essex, while Charles Arundel, subsequently having to take refuge in the Spanish embassy in Paris, would be put on an allowance by King Philip. In the meantime, however, the pair whose machinations Oxford had exposed lashed back with a fury born of desperation. Denying all accusations made against them, Arundel called them emanations of "a giddy brain" which "must dissolve to nothing now," while Howard would have "the botchie and deformities of his misshapen life suffice . . . to discredit and disgrace the warrant of his wreakful work." To Arundel, Oxford's "vices are so vile and so scandalous," embracing "all acts of cruelty, injury and villainy" that "he hath . . . damned himself to the pit of hell." The baselessness of the calumnies has not prevented their being exploited to this day by those with almost as good reason as Howard and Arundel had to blacken Oxford's character. A.L. Rowse regales us in prurient detail with an episode concocted by Arundel of Oxford and a serving-man, pointing out that a homosexual bent would disqualify Oxford as Shakespeare—a cogent enough argument but wide of its mark and conspicuously so in deriving from a time when de Vere's addiction to the opposite sex was such as to land him in jail.

It was reported that the traitors whom Oxford had exposed were put under arrest and, briefly, Oxford with them. At the same time, the French ambassador wrote a long, self-serving account to his royal master, on which history has depended for its version of events, of Oxford's "disgrace." Accordingly, it is pleasant to record that just a month after his disclosure of the perfidy of Howard and Arundel the Earl entered one of Elizabeth's great tournaments and that he defeated, among the rest, the challenger whose accession to an earldom the event was held to honor—Henry Howard's nephew Philip Howard who four years later would be convicted of treasonable activities, to spend the rest of his life in prison.

The shadow that lies unlifted across Oxford's memory, of which Grosart tells us, is cast in part by the unrestrained slander of his erstwhile associates. What accounts for far more of it, what is a major tragedy of English letters, is the control of the records of Elizabeth's reign by the Cecils, from that day to this a leading family in England. Burghley and his son Robert, later the Earl of Salisbury, were determined that no documents would survive that would reflect unfavorably on them in their relations with de Vere or reveal his deep involvement in activities that in their view would tarnish the family name. ("Shake-speare, we must be silent in our praise.") We have a touching and piteous letter of December 1581 from the Countess of Oxford pleading her case, and while her husband replied immediately, as we know from the carefully preserved copy of her response to that, we have no letter Oxford ever wrote her; all disappeared. We do have one of his thanking his father-in-law for his efforts to restore his standing with the Queen, however, and these were sufficiently successful to have him freed from house arrest and be re-united with his wife.

Oxford's ill fortune was not entirely over, however. In March 1582 came a sword-fight with Anne Vavasor's uncle, Thomas Knyvet, who unquestionably provoked it; we read that they "are both hurt, but my Lord of Oxford more dangerously." It is quite possible that the poet of the *Sonnets* in referring to his lameness was speaking literally. The set-to was not the end of it. Albert Feuillerat wrote in 1910, "This was the signal for war between the two houses. As at another time in Verona, the streets of London were filled with the quarreling clamors of these new Montagues and Capulets." That, of course, is an exaggeration, but there was indeed bloodshed and at least two men were killed in the clashes between Oxford's followers and Knyvet's. Oxford, Burghley would write in a letter, was in nowise responsible for "these brabbles and frays." If the events recalled *The Tragedy of Romeo and Juliet* to Feuillerat's mind, it is more than likely that they recalled to Oxford's the juvenile poem *Romeus and Juliet.* It is certain that the action in the play takes place in 1581, for the Nurse remarks in it, "'Tis since the earthquake now 11 years," her reference surely being to the quake that struck in the neighborhood of Verona in 1570. The memory of it would still have been fresh when Oxford looked up at the balcony of the palace of the Capuletti as throngs of tourists do today. The dramatist may be seen as split between Mercutio and Romeo, through whom a nascent Hamlet repeatedly speaks. ("O! teach me how I should forget to think," and "Not mad, but bound up more than a madman is;/ Shut up in prison.") And may the reader take note of what Romeo says of Rosaline, in whom we see Elizabeth—the cues are unmistakable—as Oxford saw her.

Oxford and Lyly

As early as 1577, Oxford had two "tenements" in the Savoy, once a Lancaster castle, in which deserving university students and writers could obtain lodging through an influential patron. Prominent among these was John Lyly, whose *Euphues: The Anatomy of Wit* and *Euphues and his England* were published in 1578 and 1579 respectively. The two books, in which the English novel was born, concerned the adventures of an Athenian, "a young gentleman of great patrimony" who was welcomed into the highest circle in England, Lyly's biographer, R. Warwick Bond, states, as that same circle would welcome his story. Confessing to having written nothing before, Lyly dedicated the second to Lord Oxford, whose secretary he had evidently already become. Of the first, which he candidly admitted his friends had not thought he had it in him to write, he avowed that he had "sent [it] to a Nobleman to nurse"—undoubtedly the same Earl—"who with great love brought him up for a year, so that . . . he hath his Nurse's name on his forehead." Gabriel Harvey would remind Lyly of "thy old acquaintance in the Savoy, where young Euphues hatched the eggs his elder friends laid"; further he would call Lyly the "foil [mirror] of Oxford" and, ostensibly speaking of the university but unquestionably referring to de Vere, "the fiddlestick of Oxford." Bond, devoting nine pages in small type to parallels between *Euphues* and Shakespeare, tells us that Jaques in *As You Like It* "is simply Euphues Redevivus" and goes on to proclaim that

> There was no play before Lyly. He wrote eight, and immediately thereafter England produced some hundreds—produced that marvel and pride of the greatest literature in the world, the Elizabethan drama. What the long infancy of her stage had lacked was an example of form, of art: Lyly gave it.

The reader will be in no doubt as to who I believe deserves the credit given to Lyly—as I believe future scholarship, unshackled, will see that he receives it. Even R.W. Bond acknowledges that "From the Earl, probably, it was that Lyly first received the dramatic impulse," though he fails to report that after leaving Oxford's employment, Lyly never wrote another play, or anything else of any merit. Sir Sidney Lee, terming the lyrics in Lyly's plays "their most attractive features," recognizes that "they were not published in the quartos but first" in the "collected edition of 1632." We may see a reason for the delay if we compare a song from *Merry Wives* with one from Lyly's *Endymion*:

> Pinch him, fairies, mutually;
> Pinch him for his villainy.
> Pinch him, and burn him, and turn him about,
> Till candles and starlight and moonshine be out,

> Pinch him, pinch him, black and blue,
> Saucy mortals must not view
>   What the Queen of Stars is doing,
> Nor pry into our fairy wooing
>   Pinch him blue
>   And pinch him black.
>   Let him not lack
> Sharp nails to pinch him blue and red
> Till sleep has rocked his addle head.

In 1583 Oxford acquired the sublease of Blackfriars, the theatre established in the former monastery. Blackfriars was associated with the boy players, drawn from the great church choirs that had been "at least as conspicuous as the professional companies," Sir Edmund K. Chambers writes. He adds that at this time "the [St.] Paul's boys appear to have joined . . . a composite company to which Lord Oxford's boys also contributed." Oxford transferred the lease of Blackfriars to Lyly and probably gave him direct supervision of the new boys' company acting there. The next year, two plays of Lyly's were played, before the Queen by the Queen's own children amalgamated with the children of Paul's. Oxford was the patron on both occasions as he had been when at the performance a few months earlier "by the Earl of Oxenford his boys" of a play called *Agamemnon and Ulysses*, which we may guess was an early version of *Troilus and Cressida*. In addition to his involvement in Court theatricals, Oxford had his traveling players, whose performances at this time included, perhaps portentously, some at Guild Hall in Stratford-on-Avon.

Heavy Losses, Literary Protégés

As the 1583-84 season was exciting for him in the theatre, it also brought two heavy losses. The small trading fleet to the Spanish Main to which he had evidently contributed, *Edward Bonaventure,* was routed by the Spanish and returned empty-handed. Much worse was the tragedy recorded in the burial register at Castle Hedingham: "1583. May 9th. The Earl of Oxenford's first son." The grief of the mother lives on today in four *Epitaphs* she composed of awkward but touching verse. The Queen may have been moved by the infant's death as well as by Burghley's report that his son-in-law was reduced to four servants, of whom one "waiteth upon his wife, my daughter, and another is in my house upon his daughter Bess." At any rate, an insider at Court wrote in June that the day before "the Earl of Oxford came into her [Elizabeth's] presence and after some bitter words and speeches, in the end all sins are forgiven."

To the end Oxford would be pursuing schemes for raising money, which he was better at running through than at raising. For the fourth time he obeyed the siren voice singing of Cathay and, with the Earls of Leicester and Bedford, invested in the Fellowship for the Discovery of the North West Passage—only to have the two vessels that set forth in June 1585 return in September in the belief that the entrance to the passage had been found but with nothing else by way of recompense.

Spartan as Oxford's life had become by comparison with the lives of those with whom he rubbed shoulders at Court, he yet managed to acquire at this time the huge house known as Fisher's Folly, on the present site of Devonshire Square. The purchase, however, would seem to have been more for England's sake than a self-indulgence. Not only would it come to be reported that "The Queen's Majesty Elizabeth hath lodged there," but we may believe that the house was for the accommodation of the circle of writers forming around Oxford. These we know, or have good reason to believe, included Anthony Munday, Robert Greene, Christopher Marlowe, Thomas Nashe and Thomas Kyd. Oxford became the recipient of almost worshipful dedications by Munday and Greene, who, calling Oxford "a worthy favorer and fosterer of learning," wrote "Wherever Maecenas lodgeth, thither no doubt will scholars flock." And he stated, arrestingly, "All that courted Atalanta were hunters, and none sued to Sappho but poets"; not only was Oxford a Maecenas—which Nashe also called him—but he stood to his protégés as we have observed, as the greatest of their calling.

Anthony Munday calls for special note. Having in the dedication of his *Zelauto* left no doubt of the common identity of Oxford and Euphues, his handiwork leaves little more of the common identity of Oxford and Shakespeare. "In his versatility the epitome of his age," Sidney Lee calls Munday, going on to say that of the 18 plays he had a hand in, "several were highly successful" and that these began with one "written . . . for the Earl of Oxford's company." That may have been the much mulled-over, anonymous play, *The Book of Sir Thomas More*. This has come down to posterity in manuscript, with "the original material . . . written throughout in a single hand," as E.K. Chambers states, identifying it, as do other scholars, "with Anthony Munday's." That would be natural if the play were by Oxford, whom Munday served as secretary. It would be hardly conceivable had it been the work of the "Bard of Avon," to whom orthodoxy has long attributed one unmistakably Shakespearean scene, even citing it as a demonstration of Shakspere's literacy. Now comes Thomas Merriam of Basingstoke, England, demonstrating by computer-assisted stylistic analysis and the linked usage of distinctive words that the authorship of Sir Thomas More is at one with that of *Julius Caesar, Titus Andronicus* and *King Lear*. Incidentally, Nina Green in her *Edward de Vere Newsletter* has used the criteria of distinctive words to link Oxford's early poems and his letters with Shakespeare's works. More than that, William Plummer Fowler, setting forth "consistent correspondences" in "thought and phraseology," has composed a large volume on *Shakespeare Revealed in Oxford's Letters* (1986).

Arms Versus Letters

In a fascinatingly evocative account by Leopold von Wedel of Pomerania of a tournament before the Queen of November 1584, which I refrain with difficulty from quoting at length, we read:

> On this day there were to be seen many fine horses and beautiful women, not only amongst the ladies of the Queen, but also amongst those of the gentry, nobility and burghers. The tournament lasted until five o'clock. Then my Lord Lester, the Queen's Master of the Horse, bade the knights cease from combat. The Queen then presented the prizes to the Earl of Oxenfort and to the Earl of Arundel [not to be confused with Charles Arundel], the eldest son of the Duke of Norfolk whom the Queen had beheaded

—and whom his devoted cousin, young Edward de Vere, had tried desperately to save after he had been convicted of treasonable involvement with Mary Queen of Scots.

Six months after the tournament it appeared that Oxford's dreams of military exploit were going to be realized at last. With Antwerp having fallen to the Spanish, an English field army was sent to the continent. With it went "the Guard of the Earl of Oxford," who himself went to join it. The Spanish Ambassador wrote his king of a force of about 4,000 to be sent to Zeeland of which "it was said that the leader of it would be the Earl of Oxford." Under pressure from the Dutch, the Queen had placed the expeditionary force under the Earl of Leicester. This may well have contributed to the mysterious turn of events that followed. On October 21st an agent of Elizabeth's in the Netherlands reported that "the Earl of Oxford had returned this night to England, upon what humor I know not." Typically, no communication of Oxford's on the matter survives. It may be a fair guess, however, that his humor was that of Othello's embittered "Farewell the neighing steed and the shrill trump, . . . The royal banner and all quality,/ Pride, pomp and circumstance of glorious war!"

In view of what followed, I think we may be permitted to

surmise that Elizabeth had decided that her gifted earl could serve her Majesty's person and her realm in a far more valuable capacity than any he could bring to glorious war. We may have a hint of it in an abusive letter challenging him to a duel—which Oxford would have disregarded—written him early in 1585 by a Thomas Vavasor, evidently a brother of Anne's and little more than a boy. In it the writer fears that "nothing can awake thy base and sleepy spirits" because "thou art so much wedded to that shadow of thine." Anne Vavasor would have known it had her paramour already been evolving a shadowy other self through whom to express his unacknowledgeable literary and dramatic imperatives.

In 1586, William Webbe wrote in *A Discourse of English Poetry*:

> I may not omit the deserved commendations of many honourable and noble Lords and Gentlemen in Her Majesty's Court, which, in the rare devices of poetry, have been and yet are most skillful; among whom the right honourable Earl of Oxford may challenge to himself the title of most excellent among the rest.

Three years later, the author of *The Arte of English Poesie*, believed to be George Puttenham, would write:

> I know very many noble gentlemen in the Court that have written commendably, and suppressed it again, or else suffered it to be published without their names to it: as if it were a discredit for a gentleman, to seem learned. . . . of which number is first that noble gentleman Edward Earl of Oxford.

The Deathless Years

The year 1586 may, I think, be taken as the continental divide in Oxford's life, on the far side of which his undertakings would be primarily those that would make Shakespeare the greatest name in literature. In June of that year, the Queen by Privy Seal Warrant addressed to the Exchequer directed that there be paid to "Our right trusty and well beloved Cousin the Earl of Oxford . . . the sum of One Thousand Pounds yearly;" for this, it was stated, nothing "by way of account" would be required. Probably double in value the salary of the Prime Minister today, it would far exceed any other comparable annuity granted by the notoriously tight-fisted Queen. To be renewed by King James, who spoke in connection with it of "great Oxford," it would run the duration of Oxford's life, which is to say for 18 years. The reader will not have forgotten the Reverend Dr. John Ward's reporting in 1662 that Shakespeare "supplied the stage with two plays every year, and for that had an allowance so large that he spent at the rate of £1,000 a year, as I have heard." Two times 18 is 36, just the number of plays in the first collected edition of *Mr. William Shakespeares Comedies, Histories & Tragedies*, in the First Folio of 1623.

The Elizabethan theatre was immensely popular, and evidently with Elizabeth herself no less than with the public. She saw in it, however, more than a means of entertainment. Edmund Bohun wrote in 1693 in *The Character of Queen Elizabeth* that her

> care was to restrain the license of the theatre, and she prohibited all exercises and plays but what were manly, and tended to be fitting of her subjects for war by making their bodies more hardy and active, and their souls more valiant.

She would have been especially anxious and resolved on this score in 1586 when the showdown with Spain was approaching. She would (I judge) have heard her "well beloved Cousin" bring England's past to life on the stage with riveting eloquence. The historical plays must have appalled audiences with their dramatization of the bloody costs of national disunity, of a disputed succession to the English throne—and Elizabeth's was remorselessly challenged. Only three years before, her secret service, by pouncing on Francis Throckmorton, had exposed the plan for a French or combined Spanish-Italian force to invade England and replace Elizabeth on the throne—after, certainly, beheading her—with Mary Queen of Scots and re-establish the Church of Rome. Elizabeth would have heard no less in those plays their stirring evocation of English patriotism on which she must rely to rally the spirits of her subjects to resist invasion. Hear Winston Churchill as he concludes his chapter on the Spanish Armada in *A History of the English-Speaking Peoples* with the final words of Shakespeare's *King John* that "struck into the hearts of his audience:"

> Come the three corners of the world in arms,
> And we shall shock them. Nought shall make us rue
> If England to itself do rest but true.

There are the dying John of Gaunt's paean—24 unforgettable lines—to

> This royal throne of kings, this sceptered isle,
> . . . .
> This blessed plot, this earth, this realm, this England,
> . . . .
> This land of such dear souls, this dear, dear land. . . .

Above all, perhaps, there is *King Henry the Fifth*, with Henry's irresistible appeal to the fighting spirit of his beleaguered followers as the battle of St. Crispin's Day looms:

> This story shall the good man teach his son;
> And Crispin Crispian shall ne'er go by
> From this day to the ending of the world,
> But we in it shall be remembered;
> We few, we happy few, we band of brothers. . . .

That *King Henry the Fifth* was initially produced when England stood in greatest peril from Spain, I venture with others to believe. Accordingly it gives one a peculiar satisfaction that the play should have been given its greatest production ever, on the screen with Sir Laurence Olivier, in World War II when British nerves were strained in mortal combat with another ruthless continental power. Oxford surely invested something of himself in Prince Hal, crony of Falstaff and other lowborn regulars of the Boar's Head, and the newly crowned Henry might have been Oxford answering charges brought against him in declaring

> And we understand him well,
> How he comes o'er us with our wilder days,
> Not measuring what use we made of them.

. . . the scenes in the Boar's Head being but one of those uses. That Fluellen in the play is simply a re-enactment of Sir Roger Williams, who fought beside Sir Francis Vere against the besieging forces of the Duke of Parma in 1587, there can be no doubt. Both captains were from Monmouthshire, and Fluellen speaks just as Sir Roger does in his book on the campaign; even the *Dictionary of National Biography* draws the parallels. And Sir Roger, we learn from Sir Francis, was a follower of Oxford's.

The foregoing does not mean I believe that Oxford's pen

was for hire by the Crown. Far from it. Genuine artists do not so much choose their subjects as their subjects choose them. And at this time Oxford would seem to have undertaken to give his own, naked story dramatic form. In 1589 Thomas Nashe would refer to "whole *Hamlets* . . . of tragical speeches". The orthodox scholar Andrew S. Cairncross believes that Shakespeare's play must have been written by then, as he and others find a reference to preparations for meeting the Spanish Armada in Marcellus's lines beginning

> **Why such impress of shipwrights, whose sore task**
> **Does not divide the Sunday from the week?**

From this and other strong indications one deduces that *Hamlet* had been introduced by 1586, though how much it resembled the play we know is impossible to guess.

This was the year, too, of the exposure by Sir Francis Walsingham of another plot against Elizabeth's life, the chief agent this time being Anthony Babington. Papers seized in Mary Queen of Scots' quarters were sufficiently incriminating. (She had been under restraint at Tutbury Castle in Staffordshire, to which her plotting in Scotland had led, since 1568.) It was Oxford's hard lot to have to sit among the commissioners who, under Burghley's leadership, had little choice but to condemn her. For Elizabeth the agony of contemplating the fate to which she must consign a fellow queen was protracted and all but unbearable. That it fell to Burghley's lot to sign the death warrant almost finished him with her and evidently created new strains in his relations with Oxford whose compunctions in the matter would have equaled Elizabeth's; and he had been through the ordeal once before with Norfolk. It is not a point I would argue (or that I am by any means the first to make), but I entreat the reader sometime to turn to Act IV, Scene 1, of *The Merchant of Venice* (surely the play called *The Jew* by a commentator in 1579 and plainly referred to by Edmund Spenser in that same year) and re-read Portia's immortal speech beginning "The quality of mercy is not strained":

> **'Tis mightiest in the mighty. It becomes**
> **The thronèd monarch better than his crown. . . .**
> **But mercy is above the sceptred sway;**
> **It is enthronèd in the hearts of kings. . . .**

Then let the reader ask himself if the appeal—which would have been a later interpolation in the play—is not couched in terms more suited to a plea to Elizabeth on Mary's behalf than to a supplication to a vengeful, bloody-minded usurer, from whom no mercy could be expected and none would be required anyway to "season justice," as Portia urged. And would not the case be strengthened if Elizabeth was meant to recognize herself (as Samuel Johnson would do two centuries later) in the eloquent, keen-witted speaker, the "rich heiress" sought as a prize by foreign suitors?

After a quarter-century, the highly unnatural bond, so trying to each, between Burghley and his son-in-law, first forged when young Edward became his ward, was greatly weakened in June 1588, with the death of the pitiable daughter of the one and wife of the other. The lifelike, recumbent effigies of Lady Anne and her mother, Lady Mildred Burghley, may be seen today on the tomb contrived for them (with a self-serving text) by Lord Burghley in Westminster Abbey, with the Oxfords' surviving offspring—three daughters—represented kneeling beside them in prayer.

That same month of June saw the Armada Philip II was to launch against England assembled in Spain, and Oxford, whatever his state of mind, had to make ready the vessel he meant to take into battle against it. Presumably this was the same *Edward Bonaventure* he had contributed to Edward Fenton's ill-starred venture to the Spanish Main in 1582. (Incidentally, the same vessel would take part in an expedition to the East Indies returning from which in 1594 one of the three vessels would be wrecked on Bermuda; and this would be related in Richard Hakluyt's *Voyages* 11 years before William Stracey's report of a wreck on the island of 1610, on which Stratfordians insist *The Tempest* must have drawn.) On July 19th, William Camden wrote in his *Annales*

the English came within ken of the Spanish Armada, built high like towers and castles. . . . The Queen forthwith commands more ships to the sea, whereupon, in voluntary manner, the Earls of Oxford, Northumberland and Cumberland, Sir Thomas Cecil, Sir Robert Cecil, Sir Walter Raleigh . . . and many other honorable personages were suddenly embarked, committing themselves to the sudden chance of war.

We read how "De Vere,"

> Like warlike Mars upon the hatches stands,
> His tusked Boar 'gan foam with inward ire,
> When Pallas filled his breast with warlike fire.

(The boar was the Oxfords' armorial crest. The evocation of Pallas again is notable.) The English "with incredible courage" had closed with the Invincible Armada by July 26th. But alas for Oxford. The next day he is reported to have withdrawn. Why? As usual, no word survives of his side of the events. Was his ship disabled? It is hard not to believe that ill success in almost all other ventures was the price Oxford paid for the brilliance of his trajectory across the literary skies; and for this, too, life's implacable balance of accounts would see to it that he would—heretofore, certainly—be denied the credit. At least we learn from a ballad of the time that in a royal procession to Saint Paul's celebrating the victory over the Armada that "The noble Earl of Oxford then High Chamberlain of England,/ Rode right before Her Majesty, . . ." who "by two noblemen along the Church was led,/ With a golden canopy o'er her head," and "The Earl of Oxford opening the windows for her Grace"—which takes us to Sonnet 125 and "Were't ought to me I bore the canopy."

From now on Oxford would be out of the public eye, as far as the record shows. His whereabouts and movements remain generally obscure to us, though we know he had had to part with Fisher's Folly along with Vere House, his home in Oxford Place. His last 15 years we may suppose he spent largely in writing or, in most cases, rewriting, the poems and plays we know as Shakespeare's. He may have spent part of his time in the manor house of Stoke Newington, which would be his home after his second marriage. He may have repaired to the valley of the Avon. In Billesley Hall, some three miles from Stratford, there is a room known as the Shakespeare room, in which, rumor has it, *As You Like It* was written—and Billesley had for 400 years been in the Trussel family, to which Oxford's maternal grandmother belonged. One property that this lady, wife of the 15th Earl of Oxford, willed to her grandson, Edward, was Bilton Manor, which overlooks the valley of the Avon near Rugby and the Forest of Arden.

Time of Writing of the Plays

Apart from those we have already mentioned, Shakespearean plays produced by the end of 1591—and I quote from orthodox scholars—include all three parts of *King Henry the Sixth*, *The Comedy of Errors*, *Titus Andronicus*, *Julius Caesar*, *King John*, *Othello*, *Macbeth*, *King Lear* and perhaps *Romeo and Juliet* and *The Taming of the Shrew*, while two such scholars add that there is no proof that *Two Gentlemen of Verona* and *All's Well That Ends Well* had not appeared by then. Most establishment scholars, I readily acknowledge, would take strong exception to such a listing.

Orthodoxy is in a bind with respect to the dating of Shakespeare's plays. Even its diehards have to admit that these had begun appearing by 1588, necessitating Shakspere's having arrived in London before then, though the first report of the presence there of their man—one "William Shakspare"—is in 1596. Luckily for academe, I should say, records of stage-performances before the 1590s are exceedingly skimpy. That does not, however, relieve the establishment of a much worse problem. By assigning dates to the plays to conform with the Stratfordian's they are compelled to have Shakespeare a late-comer, to have the greatest creative and innovative mind in our literature a follower of half-a-dozen lesser playwrights instead of their inspiration and pathfinder, as he assuredly was. "From the first, Prof. A.L. Rowse intones, "Shakespeare was a magpie, picking up pieces from everywhere." Louis Auchincloss joins the chorus in a recent work, saying that if you read the plays of Shakespeare with those of his contemporaries, "you will be struck by how closely he followed the fashion of the day." So much was Shakespeare "under the influence of Marlowe," to hear Mr. Auchincloss tell it, that "he called [Marlowe] his shepherd" and so under the influence of the Faith is Mr. Auchincloss that he puts words in Shakespeare's mouth that Shakespeare would never have dreamed of uttering.

Future scholarship, we need not doubt, will find that many of Shakespeare's plays, certainly in their original form, appeared much earlier than Shakspere could possibly have written them, even if he had come to London in 1588, as a 24-year-old. To combat the evidence that they came along very much as would be expected if Oxford were their author, the professors never tire of declaring that some of the best were written after Oxford's death. Such evidence as they present that this is so has been shown to be baseless. (Should a reference to an event subsequent to 1604 be discovered in one of the plays it would surely have been inserted "for topical effect during a revival," in Ivor Brown's words.) That a dozen plays of Shakespeare's are not heard of until after Oxford's death is true, as three are not until seven years after Shakspere's. As we have seen, the poet of the *Sonnets*, in Number 107, which refers unmistakably to events of 1603 and was certainly written no later, confesses that "death to me subscribes," a statement he would certainly not have let stand had he been alive in 1609 when *Shake-speares Sonnets* were published. That is the form of title (rather than "Sonnets by William Shake-speare") conventional· with the work of a deceased author. There is other, indisputable evidence that the poet was in fact dead. He had no hand in the publication of the intimately revealing sequence. The contents were not proofread and the dedication had to be supplied by the printer. In it "T.T.," as he signed it, referred to "our ever-living poet," the term being one never applied to a still-living person. (What would the reader make of it if at a party the host raised his glass to him and proposed a toast to "our ever-living friend"?)

Oxford, a.k.a. "Willy" and "Will," Favorite of the Muses

In 1590 Edmund Spenser published his *Fairie Queen*. The enormous work was preceded by a dozen tributes to Spenser in verse by leading poets of the time, most signed with initials. The last, its four stanzas in the verse-form of *Venus and Adonis*, is by "Ignoto," who pretty clearly was Oxford; it was to be unmistakably and amusingly echoed by Ben Jonson in the opening of his poetical tribute to Shakespeare in the First Folio. The tributary poems are followed by sonnets addressed by Spenser to leading figures around the Queen. One is addressed to the Earl of Oxford, strengthening our impression that Ignoto was he. It tells us that

> . . .the love which thou dost bear
> To th' Heliconian imps, and they to thee:
> They unto thee, and thou unto them, most dear.

Mount Helicon was the home of the Muses, and one meaning of "imp" is "Scion (esp. of a noble house)" (Oxford Universal Dictionary).

Can it be otherwise than that Spenser is calling Oxford the most beloved of all of the Muses? (Oxford, we may recall, had been declared "one whose infancy, from the beginning, was ever sacred to the Muses." That was in the dedication of a popular work by the quaintly named Angel Day, in 1586.) In another poem of 1590, *Teares of the Muses*, Spenser invoked the Muses themselves as witnesses to the sorry state to which the arts had fallen. In two stanzas that have long commended the attention of students of Elizabethan drama, the Muse of Comedy laments:

> And he, the man whom nature self had made,
> To mock herself, and truth to imitate,
> With kindly counter under mimic shade,
> Our pleasant Willy, ah! is dead of late.

Commentators beginning with John Dryden have recognized that the stanzas could apply only to William Shakespeare, with the dramatist's first biographer, Nicholas Rowe, having pointed out in 1709 that "Mr. Spenser does not mean that he was really dead, but only that he had withdrawn from the public." But, as E.K. Chambers muses, "If Shakespeare had written any comedies by 1590, of which there is no proof and little probability, he was at the beginning of his career and not, in a literary sense, 'dead.'" We may leave orthodoxy to ponder the question of how a Shakespeare could have withdrawn from the public when he had never been before it. For us it is evidence that Oxford—"under mimic shade"—was now known to his literary companions by a name that would expunge differences of class between them, the "Will" that the poet of the *Sonnets* would call himself. We have another indication three years later when Thomas Nashe, speaking of the dinner of "Rhenish wine and pickled herring" that was to prove fatal to Robert Greene, wrote that "I and one of my fellows, Will. Monox (Hast thou never heard of him and his great dagger?) were in company with him." The "great dagger," to have been worth mentioning, could well have referred to the Sword of State that pertained to Oxford as Lord Great Chamberlain.

The Groats-worth Forgery

Greene died a month after the banquet, and in less time than that there appeared *Greenes Groats-worth of Wyt*, purporting to have been written by the dying playwright. Beginning two centuries later, a very great deal was to be made over it by Shakespearean orthodoxy because of a paragraph it contains in which "R.G." warns "his Quondam acquaintance, that spend their wits in making plays," of a certain actor, an "upstart Crow, beautified with our feathers, that with his *Tygers hart wrapt in a players hide*, supposes he is as well able to bombast [fill] out a blank verse as the best of you" and "is in his own conceit the only Shake-scene in a country." That term and the line paraphrased from the play *Henry the Sixth, Part Three* have been seized upon by orthodoxy as an essential foundation of their case for Shakspere's having been an actor in London and a playwright by 1592. However, *Groats-worth* was shown by Professor Warren B. Austin in 1969, by means of painstaking computer analysis of styles, to have been the composition of Henry Chettle, a writer of plays and miscellanies, who had it printed. There is little excuse for its not having been recognized as a forgery to begin with. In its leisured, voluble, allegorical style, going on for pages and pages, it was never written by a desperate man facing death in poverty. Nashe, moreover, pronounced it "a scald trivial lying pamphlet." Acknowledging that it "is given out to be of my doing," he declared "God never have care of my soul, but utterly renounce me if the least word or syllable of it proceeded from my pen." The actor denounced in *Groats-worth* was plainly someone of vastly greater importance than a Johnny-come-lately from the provinces, someone who could not even be named. The matter comes into our story because of Chettle's expression of regret that he had offended one of the playwrights addressed by Greene whom he had subsequently found to be "no less civil than he excellent in the quality he professes" and whose "facetious [urbane, polished] grace in writing . . . approves his art." Orthodoxy identifies the offended playwright as Shakespeare, as no doubt he was, though not the Shakespeare of orthodoxy. It will be interesting to see who an unfettered (we may hope) scholarship of the future will determine the upstart Crow to have been

Oxford's Musicianship, Impecuniosity, Remarriage

In 1591 John Farmer, at one time organist and choir-master at Christ Church Cathedral in Dublin, a noted musical composer, dedicated a work in his field to Oxford, "emboldened for your

Lordship's great affection to the noble science" of music. Eight years later he would dedicate a second to the Earl, "by whose liberal hand I have so long lived" and declaring "For without flattery be it spoke, that those who know your Lordship know this, that using this science as a recreation, your Lordship have overgone most of them that make it a profession." We now, I think, can account for the love of music and wealth of musical terms in Shakespeare. There is an *Earl of Oxford's March*, said to be by William Byrd (1543-1623), and an *Earl of Oxford's Galliard*, now lost and of unknown authorship, possibly of Oxford's own.

The reverse side of Oxford's liberality was his chronic insolvency. At the end of 1591 he had been constrained to make over Castle Hedingham, the seat of his family for over four centuries, to Burghley for the upkeep of his three daughters. With Hedingham in mind it would have come readily to him to have the Fool chide the homeless King Lear with the observation that "a snail has a house . . . to put's *head in*, not to give away to his three daughters" and "He that has a house to put's *head in* has a good *head*piece."

By early 1592 Oxford had married again. His bride again was a Maid of Honour to the Queen. She was Elizabeth Trentham. Beyond her being the daughter of Sir Thomas Trentham of Staffordshire we know little about her. What is highly relevant, however, is that in February 1593 she bore her husband a son. At last, in the father's 43rd year, an heir to the Earldom had been born who would survive. The infant was christened Henry, a new name (as Edward had been) in a family of Roberts and Johns. One is drawn to the belief that the name was chosen as a compliment to Henry Wriothesley, Earl of Southampton.

Southampton and the Sonnets

Only 18 days after the christening, the narrative poem *Venus and Adonis*, with its courtly dedication to the 19-year-old youth, signed William Shakespeare, was entered in the Stationers Register (the nearest thing to copyright at that time) "under the hands of the Archbishop of Canterbury and Master Warden Stirrop"; and anyone who thinks that the salacious verses could have come through the censorship of the highest ecclesiastical authority in the land had they been the work of a mere lowly actor may wish to rethink the proposition. Both *Venus and Adonis* and *The Rape of Lucrece*, which followed it a year later, in 1594, have been perceived by astute critics as immature works, as they doubtless were, but polished for publication and dedicated, in elegant prose, to Henry Wriothesley, Earl of Southampton, by William Shakespeare. This marked the first appearance of the name in print and the last, so far as we know, for which the author, himself, would be responsible. *Venus and Adonis* was offered as "the first heir of my invention," and "invention" can only have meant the name; a writer's product may inherit his name but hardly his inventive faculty, as the professoriat would have us believe; and certainly this finished flight of verse, of 199 stanzas, was far from being the author's first work.

"The love I dedicate to your lordship is without end. . . . What I have done is yours, what I have to do is yours, being part in all I have, devoted yours." The language of the dedication of *Lucrece* is so at one with the language in which the "man right fair" of the *Sonnets* is addressed that, together with other indications, it leaves scant doubt that Southampton was the object of the poet's devotion in both. If I may repeat: Southampton's three biographers agree that this must be so; and, further, it can only be that in declaring "Thy name from hence immortal life shall have," the poet intended to dedicate the Sonnets as well as the two long narrative poems to Southampton. We can see that those who published *Shake-spears Sonnets* in 1609 would have considered such a dedication highly indiscreet and can appreciate the printer's having gone as far as he dared in that direction in addressing the volume

TO.THE.ONLIE.BEGETTER.OF.
THESE.INSVING.SONNETS.
Mr.W.H. ALL.HAPPINESSE.
AND.THAT.ETERNITIE.
PROMISED.

BY.

OVR.EVER-LIVING.POET.

WISHETH.

THE.WELL-WISHING.
ADVENTVRER.IN.
SETTING.
FORTH.

T. T.

To have dedicated the volume to "M[aste]r H.W." would have been a dead giveaway.

The *Sonnets* tell a story far from easy to fathom and without known parallel in all literature. Constraints of space allow me to add but little to what we have already observed about the sequence. The gist of it is in Sonnet 144, which begins:

> Two loves have I of comfort and despair,
> Which like two spirits do suggest me still;
> The better angel is a man right fair,
> The worser spirit a woman colored ill.

The first 125 sonnets sound the changes on the poet's obsessive emotions about the fair youth, whom he idolizes in paternal terms, urging him in the first 17 to marry and beget issue, occasionally censuring him as a father might yet speaking of himself as being knit "in vassalage" to the youth by his "duty." The balance of the sequence of 154 sonnets reflects the poet's tortured emotions about a dark wanton, the notorious "Dark Lady," and, appallingly, her designs upon the fair youth. He can confess to her:

> For thou well know'st to my dear doting heart
> Thou art the fairest and most precious jewel.

Yet in the same sonnet, having reported that "my mistress' brows are raven black," he can exclaim that

> In nothing art thou black save in thy deeds

and go on to charge that

> To win me soon to hell my female evil
> Tempteth my better angel from my side.

The wording of the dedication of *Venus and Adonis* would indicate that the poet had come to know, or to discover the depth of his feeling for the fair youth not long before, which is to say not long before 1593. That the relationship rapidly evolved is indicated by the intimacy revealed in the dedication of *Lucrece* the next year. It was in September of that same year that *Willobie His Avisa* was published. Containing the first printed mention of "Shakespeare" apart from the signatures to the dedications, it told how, we recall, Avisa and W.S. had been lovers and how H.W., the latter's "friend Harry," aspired to a like conquest. We recall, too, that the identification of the three as, respectively, Elizabeth, William Shakespeare and Henry Wriothesley has been generally accepted. Added to this, Charlotte C. Stopes, Southampton's pioneering biographer, speaks of *Willobie* as "a translation of the friendship which resulted in the writing of the *Sonnets*"; and she is not alone in this. The boyish Southampton never, of course, aspired to the favors of the aging Queen, but we recall Barbara DeLuna's suggestion that H.W. was partly Essex; and if we take it that Avisa fills the rolls of both Elizabeth and Anne Vavasor, the Dark Lady of the *Sonnets* (Avisa=AVaSor?), with W.S. having been the lover of both, then the triangle in *Willobie* could well have been the triangle that would emerge in the *Sonnets*. The fluent versifier of *Willobie* was exploiting rumor and probably to some extent groping in the dark—very profitably.

We are left with a compelling question raised by the *Sonnets*. It is a question that is inescapable and one that traditional scholarship is resolved upon escaping at all costs, and one that is beyond the bounds of this inquiry. How is it that the poet of the *Sonnets* can—as he unmistakably does—address the fair youth as an adoring and deeply concerned father would address his son and as a subject would his liege-lord?

There is the further significant question of how *Shakespeares Sonnets*, so stunningly revealing if read with understanding, got printed. A clue is offered in the publication for the first time in the same year, 1609, of Shakespeare's *Troilus and Cressida* with a preface addressed to the reader telling him he could "thank fortune for the scape it [the play] had made," contrary to "the grand possessors' wills." The reference is clearly to the highly placed guardians of Shakespeare's manuscripts. The *Sonnets* must have made a similar "scape." The preface to *T. and C.* is mysteriously captioned "A never writer to an ever reader. Newes"; and if the first words are not to be taken as "An E.Ver writer who, as such, *never was*," no one has been able to account for them.

In January 1595, Oxford's oldest daughter, Elizabeth, was married to William Stanley, the 6th Earl of Derby, in the presence of the Queen and the Court, with (according to tradition) *A Midsummer Night's Dream* being performed for the occasion. Oxford acquired a son-in-law only 11 years his junior and one with tastes and practices so congenial to his own that some have considered Derby himself as having been Shakespeare. (It is a role he came along too late and lived far too long to have filled.) The 5th Earl's acting company now became the illustrious Lord Chamberlain's players and included such stalwarts as Richard Burbage, Will Kempe, John Heminge and Augustine Phillips. The history of the company, says E.K. Chambers, "is continuous throughout Shakespeare's career and there is nothing to show that he wrote for any other company. It became dominant at Court, giving 32 performances during Elizabeth's reign." The holders of the title of Lord Chamberlain during this time were anything but men of the theatre and there seems but little doubt that Oxford, as Lord Great Chamberlain, managed the affairs of the company, which led a charmed life, never in trouble with officialdom, until the very month of his death in June 1604. (Sir Henry Irving and John Payne Collier both surmise that Shakespeare ceased acting in the summer of 1604.)

In October 1595 we find Oxford receiving from the French ambassador a letter addressed to him as Le Grand Chambellan d'Angleterre, signed Henri, expressing satisfaction "for the good offices you have performed on my behalf in her [Majesty's] presence, which I beg you to continue and believe that I will always consider it a great pleasure in whatever might bring about your personal satisfaction." This is the only hint we have of Oxford's acting in such a capacity, and it probably had to do with the French king's seeking Elizabeth's help in his nation's war with Spain.

This is almost the last we hear of what Oxford was doing. The next year he moved with his Countess to a house she had bought in Hackney, an early suburb north of London. Our hope must be that the tranquility he had sought was now his, that the Countess Elizabeth, of undivided loyalties, proved a more understanding wife than Anne had been, and that the turbulence of the two infatuations that make the *Sonnets* painful reading had subsided, enabling him to give himself to his writing and to the management of his actors undistracted. We do know this. The Lady Elizabeth wrote a wifely appeal to a judge of the High Court on her husband's behalf in the matter of a recalcitrant tenant. Further, Oxford and his son-in-law could share theatrical and musical interests and the two couples were visitors in each other's homes. However, we read that in September 1597 Oxford could not attend her Majesty at Burghley's country estate because "I have not an able body."

The year 1598 marks an historic turning-point in our chronicle. One event that made it such was the loss to Elizabeth of the outstandingly trusted and capable adviser she had had since her enthronement. William Cecil Baron Burghley of Burghley died at 78; and he died leaving wealth of staggering proportions, including 298 properties. A month afterward a death of another kind was visited upon his son-in-law. Oxford was to be lastingly deprived of his title to property infinitely more valuable, if our detective-work is sound: acknowledgment of his authorship of his nation's greatest literature—a loss that need not, however, be irreparable. That it followed hard upon Burghley's death was surely not merely coincidental. Burghley must himself, I think, have engineered it because he saw his end approaching.

Burghley had toiled through life with two ends in view: to make England great in the world and to make the Cecils great in England; and his success in both had been extraordinary. All along he had suffered the distraction of that wayward, intractable erstwhile ward and son-in-law of his, Edward. If it was through him that his granddaughters bore one of England's most illustrious and historic names—de Vere—he was none the less not going to have their issue stigmatized because the improvident, headstrong, sometimes riotous—but touchy and stiff-necked!—scion of that house had betrayed his great name by giving himself to practices proscribed for the nobility. He did so most flagrantly by writing plays that drew crowds to inn-yards and common theatres. The enthusiasm those plays evoked at Court, not least on the part of the Queen, the strengthening of the nation's sinews by the historical plays, was surely not lost on the Queen's chief councillor. Burghley may even have had an inkling that his son-in-law by his toil had succeeded as brilliantly as he in achieving lasting greatness for England, albeit it in another sphere. Well, he would not deprive posterity of a word Edward had written. He would only ensure that the one would be divorced from the other. And perhaps if he did so and if he saw to it that Edward was largely expunged from the record of Elizabeth's reign, his having consorted, even cavorted, with actors and vulgar scribes would be forgotten. (Burghley could only have shuddered at the recollection of the ballad describing the procession down to the wharves of Plymouth, led by the Queen, on Francis Drake's return from his circumnavigation of the globe, that infernal ballad with the lines "Then came the Lord Chamberlain with his white staff,/ And all the people began to laugh." The white staff was the Lord *Great* Chamberlain's.)

In his designs, the aging councillor would surely have had the unreserved support of the Queen. Elizabeth could only have been appalled by the prospect of her being recognized in her depictions in that impulsive, unreckoning genius's plays and poems as she surely would be if their authorship were known. And there were the reputations of others at stake. Was her beloved Leicester to go down in history as Claudius even as she went down as Gertrude? Could Christopher Hatton ever forgive her if the public were to see him in the self-loving Malvolio? (Mal-vol-io=Evil Will to E.O.?) Could the heirs of the lovely young poet-soldier Sir Philip Sidney contain themselves were he recognized in Boyet of *Love's Labour's*, Slender and that Aquecheek fellow? On this score Burghley's apprehension would have been as lively as the Queen's, faced as he was with the prospect of going down in history as the bumbling, prolix Polonius—as he would despite all his contriving; even the self-appointed scholastic authorities of the future would be unable to mistake that characterization, so plain was the dramatist's intent.

Up to now, according to E.K. Chambers, 14 of the plays we know as Shakespeare's had been produced or printed, all without an author being named. From 1598 on, the practice would be to attribute them to William Shakespeare. It seems evident that with Burghley facing an early end, the decision was reached to have the plays attributed to the disembodied William Shakespeare of the dedications of the narrative poems. The new order was launched unobtrusively within a month of Burghley's death in a collection of anecdotes, allusions and sayings entitled *Palladis Tamia*, by Francis Meres, a Master of Arts of Oxford and Cambridge. The author declared that "the sweet, witty soul of *Ovid* lives in mellifluous and honey-tongued *Shakespeare*, witness his *Venus and Adonis*, his *Lucrece*, his sugared Sonnets among his private friends, &c." In respect of "Comedy and Tragedy," he further announced that "*Shakespeare* among the English is most excellent in both kinds for the stage," and he listed six plays of Shakespeare's in each category. He then went on to say that "the Muses would speak with *Shakespeares* fine filed phrase if they would speak English." In the next year, incidentally, five sonnets accepted as Shakespeare's, along with 14 other poems perhaps nearly all his, were published in *The Passionate Pilgrim*. The kinship of these sonnets and of Shakespeare's 67-line poem, *The Phoenix and the Turtle*, of 1601 with *Venus and Adonis* led to speculation as long as a century ago that all reflected the story of the poet's intimate involvement with Elizabeth. Especially in view of what *Willobie* tells us, it is a subject tempting to explore but beyond the scope of this inquiry.

So far so good in turning curiosity as to the authorship of

the poems and plays in the direction of a William Shakespeare. But who was he? There had to be someone to point to if the pseudonym were not to be penetrated. If our reconstruction be valid, a canvas of the field turned up one William Shakspere (or Shakspare or Shakspyr or Shaxpere) from Stratford-on-Avon. He proved to be well suited for the role not only in having a similar name but in being not widely known in London and in being virtually illiterate and thus unable to write anything impossible to associate with literary skill. Moreover, he proved to be transportable, for a price, back to his native heath, where his laughable disqualifications for the role assigned him would not queer the game. A century later it would be reported that the Earl of Southampton gave "Shakespeare" a thousand pounds—then a huge sum— "to enable him to go through with a purchase which he had a mind to"; and no one has been able to come up with a more likely source of the astonishing investments Shakspere made in Stratford. These began with a down-payment of £60 on the second finest house in the town, in 1597, suggesting that he had already in that year been picked as a stand-in. Two of his later investments alone came to £760. The hush-money, if such it was, may well not have stopped there. Lord Oxford's second Countess, who survived him by eight years, provided in her will for quarterly payments in an unspecified amount to be paid to "my dombe man," which would certainly seem an apt designation of the cooperatively mute Stratfordian.

The Official Fiction Spurned

What must strike us at this distance of time is how slight the effort was by the schemers to associate the plays and poems of Shakespeare with the Stratfordian for it to have succeeded as it did, standing common sense on its head for generations of readers. Apparently all that was done until years after the deaths of the principals was simply to have it bruited abroad that the poet-dramatist was Will Shakspere. Even this we should not know of but for a few persons who scorned the deception. In about 1600 the students at Cambridge staged *The Return from Parnassus*, in which an actor called "Kempe" in a conversation with one called "Burbage" distinguishes between "our fellow Shakespeare" and "the university men" who "smell too much of that writer Ovid and that writer Metamorphosis and talk too much of Proserpina and Jupiter." The giveaway is of course that it was in Shakespeare of all the writers that the sweet witty soul of Ovid lived on; "People spoke of his poetry," we recall that Rowse wrote, "as that of an English Ovid." It was in Shakespeare, too, that allusion to classical figures abounded (30 to Jupiter, 50 to Diana, 23 to Neptune, 36 to Phoebus Apollo, and with Proserpine invoked in *The Winter's Tale*—evidently of 1594—in lines as charming as any in literature). Moreover, only one so ignorant as to believe Metamorphosis a writer could fail to recognize Shakespeare by the criteria cited as pre-eminently a university man.

Another who gleefully mocked the attribution of Shakespeare's plays to an unlettered man was "F.B.," accepted as having been the playwright Francis Beaumont, in a poetical letter of 1615 to Ben Jonson. Orthodox scholars have always—of necessity—had F.B. say that Shakespeare's lines were clear of all learning and "show how far a mortal man may go by the dim light of nature"; and they cite the passage as proof that the dramatist owed all his achievement to inherent genius and little if any to education. What F.B. does say, however, tongue conspicuously in cheek, is that Shakespeare's "best" lines are clear of learning, meaning that his others are not. He does not say that Shakespeare shows how far a mortal man may go by the dim light of nature but that is what "our heirs shall hear" from "preachers apt [fitted] to their auditors." Thus does F.B. neatly dispose of the official pretense.

It was in 1599 that Ben Jonson himself had dealt the imposture a devastating, if also comic, blow. This was in his play *Every Man Out of His Humour*. In it he has a character named Sogliardo complain of the "Harrots" (Heralds) that "they speak i' the strangest language, and give a man the hardest terms for his money, that ever you knew"; but "I can write myself gentleman now, here's my patent, it cost me thirty pound, by this breath." This is quite likely to have been how a coat of arms was secured in the name of William Shakspere's father, "John Shakespeare," which later got the Garter king of arms in trouble for having made grants to base persons, among them "Shakespeare." (The grant, after being twice rejected, seems to have been made in 1596. Inasmuch as the arms feature a spear in the diagonal, Will Shakspere may have started as early as that capitalizing on the similarity of his name to that of the illustrious but mysteriously disembodied poet.*) That Sogliardo is Shakspere is made unmistakable by the

* In default of anything much else to support their claims for the Stratfordian, his disciples make much of a drawing of his coat of arms bearing the legend "Shakespear ye Player by Garter." The drawing lacks a provenance, however, and the handwriting is distinctly of a later period than the Elizabethan.

motto proposed for him, this being "Not without mustard," echoing the Stratfordian's "Not Without Right." (The original application for arms having been rejected with the notation NON, SANZ DROICT, or "No, without Right," the cheeky "natural wit" converted it to his purpose by deleting the comma after NON.) Jonson describes Sogliardo as "an essential clown" who "comes up every Term to learn to take Tobacco & see new motions." Acknowledging that Sogliardo's motto is a play on "Shakespeare's," A.L. Rowse braves it out: it is all "making fun of taking out coats of arms and crests. And very good fun it is." Sogliardo "is not," E.K. Chambers assures us, " a 'portrait' of Shakespeare." Not a *portrait*, exactly. But there is no getting around it. The fraternity of scholars actually expects us to believe that Ben Jonson could have represented as a bumpkin, an "essential clown," the poet who has given us the loveliest of verse, the dramatist who has reached into human nature with unmatched understanding to create a score of deathless characters, whom Jonson called the "Soul of the Age, The applause! delight! the wonder of our stage!" whom he "lov'd on this side idolatry."

The writer, and poet, who spoke of the sadness of what was presaged in *Palladis Tamia*, and in that very year, was John Marston, a barrister of the Temple who later collaborated in a play with Ben Jonson. In his *Scourge of Villanie* of 1598, he interrupted his fulminations against mankind with these lines—and let the reader bear in mind that it was Edward de Vere's name that began and ended in the same letter:

> Far fly thy fame,
> Most, most of me beloved, whose silent name
> One letter bounds. Thy true judicial style
> I ever honour, and if my love beguile
> Not much my hopes, then thy unvalued worth
> Shall mount fair place when Apes are turned forth.

Have we not our story here in five and a half lines? Can there be any doubt as to what Marston is talking about? And shall we remain deaf to the hopes that come down to us over the centuries?

By the time of his death, "Will. Shakspere, gent." had achieved so little of his subsequent fame that in an age when copious tributes conventionally followed upon the passing of much lesser poets than Shakespeare, when on Richard Burbage's there was in London "not one eye dry," Shakspere's death went totally unremarked, so far as we know, except in the local burial record. He was moreover, held in so little regard by his fellow townsmen that his name was even omitted from his tomb. That he would be credited with the works of William Shakespeare is owing entirely to the artful ambiguities of two memorials. Both of these, we may be confident, were in their entirety the work of Ben Jonson, engaged by the authorities for that purpose. One consists of the introductory matter of the First Folio of 1623, the other of the inscription on the monument to "Shakspeare" that had been installed in the church at Stratford by 1622, and by outsiders. We know it was not by the family, as we are told to believe. Had it been, the inscription would not have had "Shakspeare" "with in this monument" when the body was at some remove, beneath the floor, and the first name, important to those who share the last, would not have been omitted.

A Monumental Jape

The inscription on the monument deserves to be quoted in full since it represents the ultimate feat of verbal gymnastics. Imagine how it could be that those acquainted with Will Shakspere could have accepted the tribute as that to their uneducated, pitilessly mercenary neighbor, the "malster and moneylender" (as James Joyce called him) of whom nothing good was ever said, that we know of, except that he had a wit, while the world at large has accepted it as a tribute to the supreme artist in words of all time, "Britain's triumph," as Jonson would say of him. We may grant that viewers in the first category were for the first century and a quarter abetted in their acquiescence by the original bust of the subject of alabaster, those in the second in theirs by its replacement of painted limestone, in 1748. An engraving of the original artifact published by Sir William Dugdale in 1656 shows a long-faced, sour-looking individual with down-drooping moustaches and arms akimbo, hands on a sack of grain. The current effigy represents a round-faced, coarse-looking man but one now with a quill pen in one hand, the other resting on a sheet of paper. The damning sack of grain could not be eliminated without flagging attention to the substitution, so it was converted to a cushion—a curious writing-surface, but what would you have? Stratfordians desperately insist that the present bust is the original, with minor restoration and that it simply was carelessly depicted in Dugdale's book. This is nonsense. The pen and paper would have struck the keynote in a depiction of a great writer, impossible to overlook, and a sack of grain would never have been imagined. In 1709, illustrating the first biography of "Shakespeare," the bust is still depicted with hands on the sack, though given a more seemly countenance.

So here is that gem of an inscription

IUDICIO PYLIUM, GENIO SOCRATEM, ARTE MARONEM:
TERRA TEGIT, POPVLVS MAERET, OLYMPUS HABET.[1]

STAY PASSENGER, WHY GOEST THOV BY SO FAST?
READ IF THOV CANST, WHOM ENVIOVS DEATH HATH PLAST
WITH IN THIS MONVMENT SHAKSPEARE: WITH WHOME,
QUICK NATVRE DIDE: WHOSE NAME DOTH DECK Y^s TOMBE.
FAR MORE THAN COST: SIEH ALL, Y^t HE HATH WRITT,
LEAVES LIVING ART, BVT PAGE, TO SERVE HIS WITT.

The locals (as the British call them) would have little trouble with the English inscription. Yes, it was likely the visitor would pass by without taking in whose monument this was: how would he have heard of Will Shakspere? "Read if thou canst": probably the "passenger" would be as illiterate as Will was. As for "all that he hath writt," that was a pretty fancy reference to Will's clownish verse.*
But that was just sort of a grand entry to the tribute to Will's famous "witt." That was what the monument was celebrating. As for the Latin gobbledygook, that was just the highflown talk of the Londoners who for some reason had made Will wealthy and were set on building him up, paying for the monument as they had—and with the mistaken notion that "Shakspeare" would be "within" it.

For their part, sophisticated outsiders coming to Stratford and expecting to find a monument commemorating the immortal

---

* A visitor to Stratford in 1634, finding "a neat monument to the famous English poet, Mr. William Shakespeare," had quoted to him as an example of the poet's work "some witty and facetious verses" about a neighbor that "the said poet did merrily fan up." As they have come down to us, these are:

"Ten in the hundred the devil allows
But Combes will have twelve he swears & avows:
If anyone asks who lies in this Tombe;
Hoh! quoth the Devil, 'tis my John o' Combe."

poet-dramatist would be able to accept what they saw as just such a memorial. They would clutch at that "sieh all that he hath writt" and would find suitable acclaim in the Latin Preamble. That assumed, of course, that the genius of Sophocles, the great Greek tragedian, would have been attributed to Shakespeare had not the graver, in his ignorance, made it the "genio Socratem." But what shall we think of the judgment of the self-acclaimed scholars? Can the occupants of the chairs of English literature have for two centuries believed that Shakespeare's contemporaries, called upon to honor the greatest of literary creators, were unable to come up with an English inscription more adequate than the nearly empty rigmarole they devised for the purpose? Can they believe it possible that a monument to William Shakespeare should not by a single word have indicated that he ever composed a play? Can they believe that the English inscription could have passed muster while failing not only to recognize him as a playwright but to so much as hint that he ever indited a line of verse? Do they not find it singular that even in the Latin the only such suggestion is in the obscure *arte Maronem*? They must know that Shakespeare would never have been called a Virgil in art when his kinship with Ovid was famous. Can the scholars not see, however, that had the genius of Sophocles and—undisguisedly—the art of Ovid been attributed to the "Shakspeare" of the monument, even his more astute fellow villagers would have recognized that he was being identified as the William Shakespeare who was supreme among writers and the monument have been a laughingstock? (Ben Jonson was a sly one.)

How, in a word, can the professors have looked at the monument while having read the record as we have been over it and yet hold out to the bitter end that Shakespeare's poems and plays were the work of Stratford's maltster and money-lender? However it may be explained, we should not forget what it tells us of the power of intellectual authority, however irrational.

The First Folio

The "notoriety . . . which the memory of William Shakespeare has brought to Stratford," says the *Encyclopaedia Brittannica*, "sprang into strong growth only towards the end of the 18th century." Whether it would have sprung into growth at all without the First Folio is hard to know. This monumental edition of MR.

WILLIAM SHAKESPEARES COMEDIES, HISTORIES & TRAGEDIES was brought out in 1623 at obviously very considerable cost. This, it is a safe bet, was borne by "the Most Noble and Incomparable Pair of Brethren," to whom the first of two dedicatory letters was addressed. (Though these were signed by the actors John Heminge and Henry Condell, no one, I think, doubts that they were written by Ben Jonson.) The brothers were the Earl of Pembroke and the Earl of Montgomery. The latter had married Oxford's daughter Susan while the former had sought the hand of her sister, but the planned marriage fell through. The title-page bore the famous engraved portrait by Martin Droeshout, unlabeled. It is reproduced more often than any other as a likeness of the dramatist, despite its look of the phony and of the impression it makes on many, the painter Gainsborough having declared: "Damn the original portrait. I never saw a stupider face." (Ivor Brown wails, "It is as bad as the effigy in the church," which he calls "that of a 'pudden'-headed William who could never have written anything except a note of hand to buy malt.")

The plays in the Folio are preceded by tributes to the dramatist by four poets, the note struck in all being that he will live forever—tributes so unstinting in their praise as to make it all the more striking that not one of Shakespeare's such worshipful fellows found two words to utter on Will Shakspere's death. (It is noteworthy, too, that all four poems prefix William Shakespeare's name with the respectful "Master," abbreviated or spelled out.) The encomium by Ben Jonson *To the memory of my beloved, The Author Mr. William Shakespeare and what he hath left us*, consists of 40 rhymed couplets, from which I have already quoted. It is doubtful that any writer has ever inspired such a eulogy from a contemporary himself so illustrious. To this day I cannot read unmoved the climactic line:

> But stay, I see thee in the Hemisphere
> Advanced and made a Constellation there!
> Shine forth, thou Star of Poets

Judging from the results, it can only be, I think, that William and Philip Herbert, respectively the Earls of Pembroke and Montgomery, and both close to Oxford, agreed upon engaging Ben Jonson to serve as impresario of the great Folio and upon their instructions to him. He was to imply that William Shakespeare was the Stratfordian in order to satisfy the authorities, but his concession to them would be minimal. Further, it was either the two sponsors' idea or they concurred in Jonson's adroit balancing act, that the credit given the Stratfordian with one hand would be withdrawn with the other. The results, the reader who bears with me will find, are instructive.

One. In an introductory verse "To the Reader," stating that that unnamed cartoon of a portrait by Droeshout "was for gentle Shakespeare cut," Jonson would cast marked doubt upon it as a likeness.

Two. In the dedicatory letter to the two Earls, the two actors Heminge and Condell, would be represented as speaking of "So worthy a Friend & Fellow as was our SHAKESPEARE," fitting the name to an actor on their own level* . . . But, unmistakably referring to their claim, Jonson would dismiss it in his tribute to his beloved, the Author: it was "as [if] some infamous bawd or whore,/ Should praise a Matron. What could hurt her more?"

Three. Jonson would apostrophize the author as "Sweet Swan of Avon". . . But not only are there three considerable Avons in England (the name meaning simply "river" in Celtic), but Lord Oxford's manor of Bilton overlooked Stratford's Avon.

Four. Jonson would address the author with the line "And though thou hadst small Latin and less Greek. . . ." But the statement—one of the most mischief-making ever written in English—when turned over in the mind proves to be one of Jonson's cagiest examples of doublespeak. That it is followed by the subjunctive "I would not [seek for names to honor thee but call forth the Greek and Roman masters]" rather than the declarative "I shall not" indicates that Jonson was using "though" in the sense of "even if." ("Though I speak with the tongue of men and of angels. . . .") If the line be taken to mean, as Stratfordians habitually do take it to mean that Shakespeare was deficient in the classical languages its absurdity is manifest. A familiarity with Latin and Greek works surfaces characteristically in Shakespeare's own; and a platoon of other writers, picked at will, would not together have contributed to the English language half so many words of Latin root. Prof. T.W. Baldwin, as we have seen, required two volumes to account for the education in Latin Shakespeare must have had while soberly entitling them—the reader won't believe this—*Shakespeare's Small Latine and Lesse Greek.*

* A bequest "to my fellows John Hemynge Richard Burbage [who had died in 1619] & Henry Condell" for the purchase of rings had been thoughtfully interlined in Shakpere's will.

Five. L[eonard]. Digges in commemorative verses would speak of "thy *Stratford* Moniment". . . . But he would do so only as one that "Time" would "dissolve" [while the generality of readers would probably think of the Stratford north of London, only a couple of miles from the Oxfords' home in Hackney].

Six. In "The Names of the Principal Actors in all these plays" immediately preceding the plays themselves, "William Shakespeare" would come first, ahead even of such super-stars as Burbage and Kempe, not to mention 23 others. . . . But everyone would know that according him such status was wholly unwarranted [even Shakspere's most enthusiastic biographers stopping short of claiming such eminence for him on the stage]. Would the listing, then, amount to outright prevarication? Not if it be in accordance with rank and the "Shake-speare" who "played kingly parts in sport" were a member of the nobility.

All this about the Folio has doubtless been tedious going for the reader. However, it has been necessary if we are to see the supports of the Stratford case for what they are, in their entirety. Moreover, there is a question arising from the Folio I shall venture to leave with the reader, for his consideration.

The only person of whom we know to have reported seeing the Stratford monument before the issuance of the Folio was an Oxford student, William Basse, who in a poem of 1622 called upon Spenser, Chaucer and Beaumont to make room for Shakespeare in their "three-fold tomb." Ben Jonson in his encomium addressed himself directly to Basse's proposal, stating that "I will not lodge thee by Spenser, Chaucer or . . . Beaumont." And why? Because

> **Thou art a Moniment, without a tomb,**
> **And art alive still, while thy Book doth live**
> **And we have wits to read, and praise to give.**

Why, because his "book" was deathless, could Shakespeare not be interred in Westminster Abbey? In what sense was he a monument without a tomb? I cannot recall seeing the professors' answers to these questions. Is it not possible that we have here, again, the case of . . . *a never writer?*

Turning back now to that never writer:

The dramatist hints broadly at Shakspere-Sogliardo's role in the proceedings in several plays. In *The Taming of the Shrew* an Induction having nothing to do with the play itself tells how an unnamed lord and his hunting-party come upon a beggar asleep on the road. The "loathsome" spectacle suggests an experiment. The lord proposes that the fellow be

> conveyed to bed,
> Wrapped in sweet clothes, rings put upon his fingers,
> A most delicious banquet by his bed,
> And brave attendants near him when he wakes,

and in all ways be treated as if he were the lord himself: "would not the beggar then forget himself?"

The beggar, who describes himself as Christopher Sly, "old Sly's son, of Burton-heath," says "Ask Marian Hacket, the fat ale-wife of Wincot, if she know me not." Burton-in-the-Heath was where Shakspere's aunt and uncle lived, and his mother was Mary Arden of Wilmcote, probably pronounced much like Wincot. If these details are not supplied to identify Christopher Sly (the sly fellow who bore the Lord?), why are we given them? The oaf declares that "the Slys . . . came in with Richard Conqueror" (and Ivor Brown tells us that "The Ardens . . . were lordly people indeed, pre-Conquest notables, accepted by William the Conqueror"). He says he is "by education a card-maker," cards being used in the combing of wool, in which Will Shakspere's father was a dealer. And the experiment works. Sly does forget himself and imagines he is the lord—as Shakspere may have allowed himself to be taken for Shakespeare by the credulous. ("When invited to writ[e], John Aubrey would recall of "Shakespear" in 1681 in his *Brief Lives*, "he was in pain"). . . . After the Induction, of two skits, the play itself, *The Taming of the Shrew*, is presented as for the entertainment of the self-imagined lord,. . . . who is found nodding at the end of the first scene. " 'Tis a very excellent piece of work," Sly exclaims. "Would 'twere done!"

In *Henry the Fourth, Part Two*, a William Vizor of Woncot—the symbolism is obvious—is introduced out of a clear blue sky to be termed "an arrant knave" though "he shall have no wrong." *As You Like It* brings us another William, an unlearned country wit who is brought in for a scene with Touchstone, "the fool who hath been a courtier" (the dramatist in whimsical mode) for the sole apparent purpose of having it indicated, in connection with "verses [that] cannot be understood," that William has received credit for that which was Touchstone's. As Touchstone says, "Now, you are not ipse [i.e. the master] for I am he." (Please see *The Mysterious William Shakespeare*, p. 748.) It tells us much about the orthodox scholars that they are content to believe that the dramatist would choose to bestow his own given name on those two Williams, one "an arrant knave," the other a country-fellow who is likened to a glass that is filled with drink only because a cup has been emptied into it.

Some Gratifications for Oxford

It was in 1599 that the organist and composer John Farmer dedicated his book of *English Madrigals* to Oxford, speaking of "your honourable mind that so much have all liberal sciences" and "your judgment in music." The Earl of Derby's proficiency in music is attested by his "Pavin made for the Opharion," published in 1624. At about this time, moreover, a letter from a Jesuit was intercepted reporting that "The Earl of Derby is busied only in penning plays for the common players." Derby had his own acting company, and we find his Countess appealing to her uncle Robert Cecil "that the company not be barred from their accustomed playing, in maintenance whereof they have consumed the better part of their substance." And she explained "for that my Lord taketh delight in them, it will keep him from more prodigal courses." The Countess of Derby was of course Oxford's daughter Elizabeth, and we can hear her wailing, "not my husband, too!"

As for her father, he was doubtless once again, the plague having abated, deeply involved in the theatre. Moreover, as Muriel C. Bradbrook writes in *The Rise of the Common Player,* "The Earl of Oxford had persuaded the Queen to tolerate a third troupe [in addition to the Lord Chamberlain's and the Admiral's], his own men combined with Worcester's." These "the Council assigned to the Boar's Head" as the place they "do best like of."

Once again one builds on the shared, absorbing interests of the two Earls and on their reported visits back and forth to warrant hopes that Oxford had found ease of mind at last, realizing, too, its essential ingredient: conjugal married contentment. In this spirit, one takes pleasure in reading a letter Oxford received in 1599 written in French by the 17-year-old son of his sister Lady Mary Willoughby. Robert Bertie wrote from the Continent with deep affection of the eternal service he had vowed "to you and your house" and of his readiness to "receive your commands with such devotion that all my life I shall be your very humble servant." Most interestingly, he adds that he would have written earlier had he found a *"subject assez digne de vous divertir de vos plus serieux affaires."*

The Fatal Essex Rebellion

Serenity of mind was not, however, long to be Oxford's lot. Early in 1601 there occurred a disastrous event from which he would perhaps not fully recover and that would prove more than the Queen could survive. The precipitator was Robert Devereux, Earl of Essex. Thirty-three years younger than Elizabeth, he was the last of the courtiers whose charm, vitality and grace captivated the Queen. He was, however, dangerously temperamental and proved insubordinate, actually laying his hand on the hilt of his sword during an interview in which his behavior provoked her Majesty into slapping him, as she once had slapped the Countess his mother.*

Unfortunately for him, the Earl of Southampton had found Essex a kindred spirit since youth, and he had taken part in two of Essex's naval campaigns against the Spanish. Elizabeth had been characteristically infuriated when her favored courtier had married Sir Philip Sidney's widow, and then, when later Southampton incurred her wrath by marrying Elizabeth Vernon, whom he had got with child, the Queen had them both thrown briefly into the Fleet prison. The two Earls were together in an Irish campaign of which Essex made a mess, even disobeying orders. Returning, Essex on February 7th madly marched through London at the head of 300 swordsmen to rally the populace—which remained mildly bewildered—against the Queen. In this, Southampton would later protest that they had acted in self-defense against "those atheists and caterpillars . . . that laid plots to bereave us of our lives." Oxford was compelled to serve on the tribunal that tried the two men. We can imagine the agony it was for him. For barefaced treason, the two Earls could only be sentenced to death. It need not surprise us, perhaps, that Southampton's sentence was commuted to imprisonment for life. As for Essex, the Queen went through all the torments she had with Mary Queen of Scots before the sentence was carried out.

The episode has always been of interest to Shakespeareans because the plotters had paid the Lord Chamberlain's men to per-

---

* That Shakespeare's Queen Margaret slaps the Duchess of Gloucester. pretending to mistake her for a servant, when the Duchess is seeking to supplant her on the throne, is sufficient to persuade Louis Auchincloss that the dramatist was ignorant of royal behavior indeed revealing "himself as bit of a hick." To Mr. Auchincloss, the scene disposes of the "peculiarly idiotic" theory that Shakespeare's plays show "an intimate familiarity . . . with court life."

form the "old play", *Richard the Second*, on the eve of the insurrection "in the hope that the play-scene of the deposition of a king might excite the citizens of London to countenance their rebellious design." Sir Sidney Lee comments: "it seems that the fascination the drama had for Southampton and his friends led them to exaggerate the influence it was capable of exerting"—though in fact the performance was clearly not given. The scheme, however, played an important part in the trial, with the name Shakespeare never being mentioned in connection with it. Nor was it by Elizabeth in her bitter remarks on the play six months later. "I am Richard II, know ye not that?" she demanded. And, with what can only have been the dramatist in her mind, she exclaimed, "He that will forget God"—a phrase Burghley had used of his son-in-law—"will also forget his benefactors; this tragedy was played 40^{tie} times before the public."

Her last favorite proved as fatal to Elizabeth as she had to him. Of her final illness, Bohun wrote: "Yet after all, her mind was more afflicted than her body; she was night and day troubled with a sorrowful remembrance of her late executed Earl of Essex." She died on 24th March 1603.

"The mortal moon hath her eclipse endured," we read in Sonnet 107, chronicling the events of that year. "And peace proclaims olives of endless age": a reference to King James's accession to the throne, presaging peace with Spain at last. There was "my true love"—the fair youth—"Supposed as forfeit to a confined doom." But now, James having released Southampton, "My love looks fresh, and Death to me subscribes." But death cannot triumph over such a poet as he, and he shows he knows it in a promise to the youth:

> . . . Spite of him, I'll live in this poor rhyme,
> While he insults o'er dull and speechless tribes;
> And thou in this shall find thy monument
> When tyrants' crests and tombs or brass are spent.

At Once Prospero and Hamlet

One is glad that in Oxford's last known letter he can offer his brother-in-law his "simple yet hearty thanks" for his help in recovering for him his ancestral Forest of Essex and say:

I do well perceive how your Lordship doth travail for me in this cause of an especial grace and favor, notwithstanding the burden of more importunate and general affairs.

Unless we are much mistaken as to who he was, Oxford spent the last year of his life—of which nothing is on record—making final revisions in the plays and writing *The Tempest*. In the summer of 1602, Bartholomew Gosnold had returned from an expedition that had explored the island-coast of Massachusetts. He had named Cape Cod, Martha's Vineyard and the Elizabeth Islands. Exactly 300 years later, Edward Everett Hale pointed out striking similarities between Gosnold's description of Cuttyhunk and Shakespeare's of the island in *The Tempest*. These would be recapitulated by J. Donald Adams in the *New York Times Book Review*, of which he was editor: There are no tropical allusions in Shakespeare's play, no palm-trees [though one appears in *As You Like It*]. Gosnold's "Meadows very large and full of green grass" become Shakespeare's "How lush . . . the grass looks, how green." Gosnold's seabirds "which did breed upon the cliffs" become Caliban's promise to "get thee young sea-mews from the rocks." Mussels, nuts and crabs appear in both. As Adams shows, "the parallels are numerous and specific." This is of special interest to us in that Gosnold's expedition was sent out by the Earl of Southampton, in whose home, as Adams suggests, the dramatist might well have met the voyagers. From their account of Cuttyhunk plus his recollection of Henry May's shipwreck on Bermuda *The Tempest* may have taken shape in his mind, though Prospero's island had to be in the Mediterranean. I might add that A.J. Cairncross gives 1604 as the probable date of *The Tempest*, while Chambers acknowledges that *Die Schöne Sidea* of 1605 by a playwright of Nürnberg conspicuously parallels Shakespeare's play.

That Prospero is the author himself making a final appearance, I think there is little dispute. With the magic he commands he is the ruler of the island, a place of haunting illusions. It is, indeed, the Theatre, in which "strange shapes" may enter "bringing in a banquet, and dance about it." These shapes, moreover, enact a play of Ceres, Iris and Juno. The magician's genius, the ethereal spirit Ariel, through whom he exercises his craft, holds captive with his enchantments even the brutish Caliban, who seems to represent the uncouth multitude. Then, among the ship's party landed on the island is the drunken lout Stephano, in whom, it becomes evident, Christopher Sly is making another appearance. This time he assumes the lord's garments to imagine himself master of the lord's estate. He is, however, exposed by Ariel, and Caliban has his eyes opened, declaring

> . . . what thrice-double ass
> Was I to take this drunkard for a god
> And worship this dull fool.

Prospero's recovery of his Dukedom, which he had lost to a usurper, may be connected with Oxford's recovery of his family's ancient holding of the Forest of Essex. It may well speak more pointedly, however, of his hope of recovering title to the poems and plays to which he had given all that was in him.

We recall how in his *Sonnets* the poet rues that "I, once gone, to all the world must die" and "My name be buried where my body is." (The reason why the "Bard of Avon" should foresee oblivion as his lot while his verse would be read "So long as men can breathe, or eyes can see," has not been vouchsafed to us.) Yet we may hope that Oxford felt confident that the origin of his works was so transparent, the hints dropped so broad, that recognition of their authorship must come. He can hardly have foreseen that the governing intellectuals of the future would be so resolute in their social rectitude as to have their eyes sealed to the evidence of the poet-dramatist's aristocratic background and to be ready to denounce as snobs all those unable to overlook it.

In *The Tempest*, the dramatist recognizes that the time has come to make an end. In lines that will forever haunt us, he declares:

> Our revels now are ended. These our actors,
> As I foretold you, were all spirits and
> Are melted into air, into thin air:
> And, like the baseless fabric of this vision,
> The cloud-capped towers, the gorgeous palaces,
> The solemn temples, the great globe itself,
> Yea, all which it inherit, shall dissolve
> And, like this insubstantial pageant faded,
> Leave not a rack behind. We are such stuff
> As dreams are made on, and our little life
> Is rounded with a sleep.

Prospero's last words (short of the Epilogue) are to "My Ariel": "Be free, and fare you well."

In *Hamlet*, in which we may believe its author kept his hand until near the end, he bids us another kind of farewell, not as the magician this time but as the man he was. In very nearly his dying words, Hamlet pleads:

> O good Horatio, what a wounded name
> (Things standing thus unknown) shall live behind me!
> If thou didst ever hold me in thy heart,
> Absent thee from felicity awhile,
> And in this harsh world draw thy breath in pain,
> To tell my story.

We may surmise that it was Edward de Vere's cousin, Sir Horace Vere, who in the year of Edward's death arranged to have *Hamlet* printed from the author's manuscript (a novelty in the case of a play of Shakespeare's) with "Head-title under ornament with royal arms" (Sir E.K. Chambers), as befitted the passing of a prince. Given the strictures of secrecy by which he was bound, it was probably the best he could do to see that his cousin's story was told.

The rest is up to us.

TO OBTAIN ADDITIONAL COPIES OF

The Man Who Was Shakespeare

See your favorite book store. If the book is not in stock, the store can order it from EPM or through leading wholesalers such as Ingram and Baker & Taylor.

For quickest delivery, send your UPS address and a check for $8.95 ($5.95 plus $3.00 shipping) to:

EPM Publications, Inc.
Box 490
McLean, VA 22101

Or call   1 (800) 289-2339
FAX   (703) 442-0599

Quotes on quantity discounts are also available via the same numbers.

Thank you for your interest in this important book!

About the Author

Charlton Ogburn has pursued a writer's goals in diverse fields. His *The Marauders* was hailed in *The New York Times Book Review* as "One of the noblest and most sensitive books by any American about his own experiences in war." "Pure treasure" was its reviewer's term for his *The Gold of the River Sea*, which in the *Boston Globe* was called "a novel in the grand manner" with "everything one hungers for in a long novel." Brooks Atkinson, drama critic of *The New York Times*, who thought *The Marauders* "the best war book I have ever read," wrote that "I think *The Winter Beach* is of equal merit from the literary, philosophical and natural-science points of view." The *Saturday Review* was moved by his *The Adventure of Birds* to call Ogburn "one of the best writers we have on natural history today" who is also "the author of some notable fiction" and "an authority on Shakespeare." . . . "A leading Shakespearean scholar," *Life* termed him.

Born in Atlanta in 1911, Charlton Ogburn was graduated from Harvard in 1932. In World War II he spent nearly five years in the Army including a final year in Military Intelligence. Transferring to the Department of State at the war's end, he resigned in 1957 to devote himself to writing. Foreign policy, however, has been one of the many subjects of his repeated contributions—some of them in fiction—to *Harper's*, the *Saturday Evening Post*, *American Heritage, Horizon, Smithsonian, Holiday, Reader's Digest, New Republic, The Washington Post, National Geographic* and *Harvard Magazine*, in which appeared as a cover-story the germ of his latest work: *The Mysterious William Shakespeare: The Myth and the Reality*. For increasing thousands of readers, this, his magnum opus (now in its fourth printing), establishes beyond question the true identity of the Elizabethan poet-dramatist—and with it his absorbing life-story—whom we prize above all other writers.

Since 1982 the author and his wife have lived in Beaufort, South Carolina.